Discussion
Process and Principles

Language
Solutions Inc.

Published by Language Solutions Incorporated
* 3198 Kevington * Eugene, Oregon * 97405 * USA *
Phone: 1-877-526-4765 *
www.languagesolutionsinc.com
contact@languagesolutionsinc.com
Copyright©2006 by Charles LeBeau and David Harrington

Book Design: Language Solutions/Hiroaki Kawajiri
Production: Language Solutions
Layout: Hiroaki Kawajiri
Design: Hiroaki Kawajiri
Front Cover Illustration: Ty Semaka
Inside Illustrations: Ty Semaka/Hiroaki Kawajiri
Copyediting: Chris Bartlett
Recorded at SoundMoves Studios Hollywood California

INTERNET SUPPORT
www.languagesolutionsinc.com

Student Book . . ISBN 1-929274-77-7
Teacher's Book . ISBN 1-929274-80-7
Audio CD   . . . ISBN 1-929274-79-3

Printed and bound in Singapore
10 9 8 7 6 5 4 3   09

Overview

You are probably reading this because you would like an overview of this book. And you would probably like a short, clear, pithy explanation. We can't promise that, but we will try to give you a clear map of the book in 250 words or less! So here goes...

◆ **The Big Picture:** We have divided this book into three distinct *Discussion Stages*:

> ## STAGE ONE: Discussion as Sharing
> ## STAGE TWO: Discussion as Exploring
> ## STAGE THREE: Discussion as Decision Making

◆ **The Medium View:** Each *Discussion Stage* contains two or three discussion cycles or *Discussion Loops*. A discussion enters a loop and continues around and around the loop until the discussion goal or task is achieved. Each loop is governed by a different principle. Different types of discussion require different loops or approaches.

Loop 3	Discussion Principle #3
Exploring Positions	**✳ Seek First to Understand ✳**
Loop 4	Discussion Principle #4
Searching for the Best Position	**✳ Separate People from Positions ✳**

◆ **The Close Up:** The book is divided into 7 Loops. Each Loop has 8 sections:

❶ Discussion Labs
These are carefully designed activities for students to experience for themselves key communicative skills related to the loop.

❷ Discussion Principle
Students are introduced to the Loop's Discussion Principle through two recorded discussions, one lacking the discussion principle, and the other practicing the discussion principle.

❸ Discussion Phrase Bank
The Discussion Phrase Bank provides the words and phrases that help the students achieve the goal of the discussion.

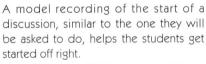

❹ Model Discussion
A model recording of the start of a discussion, similar to the one they will be asked to do, helps the students get started off right.

❺ Preparation
The preparation exercises get the students thinking about their positions before the discussion begins.

❻ Discussion Time!
The discussion topic invites a discussion of the type suggested by the Loop and the Principle of the loop.

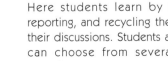

❼ Let's Continue the Discussion
Here students learn by extending, reporting, and recycling the content of their discussions. Students and teachers can choose from several options, including poster presentations, panel discussions, conference simulations, interviews, and class discussions.

Table of Contents

Table of Contents

Discussion Process and Principles

Discussion Process and Principles approaches discussion in a new way! Therefore, the book uses special terms to describe its original discussion concepts.

Process ◆ Discussion is a process that resembles a spiral with several cycles or Loops.

[Process]

Direction ◆ A discussion can go up the spiral, or down the spiral, or even skip a loop.

[Direction]

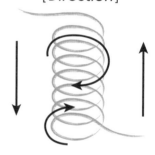

Loop ◆ Each loop is a different discussion stage. A discussion might be only one loop, several loops, or all the loops.

[Loop]

Function ◆ A function is a speech act that takes place within the loop. There are usually 3 or 4 functions unique to each loop.

[Function]

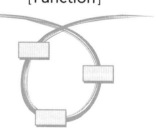

Principle ◆ Each loop is governed by a principle that should direct the behavior of the speakers and the listeners.

[Principle]

✳ **Respect Every Voice** ✳

✳ **Seek First To Understand** ✳   ✳ **Celebrate All Ideas** ✳

✳ **Know All Your Criteria** ✳

✳ **Separate People From Positions** ✳   ✳ **Look To Your Values** ✳

✳ **Uncover Your Assumptions** ✳

Read this before turning the page

This is your first discussion. At the end of this discussion, you will do an initial self-assessment of your discussion ability. At the end of the book, you will do a second self-assessment to check your discussion ability. You will be able to check your progress by comparing your initial self-assessment to your final self-assessment.

◆ *Instructions*

1. Your teacher will explain the discussion background on page 2.
2. You will have 15 minutes for part 1 of the discussion.
3. You will have 15 minutes for part 2 of the discussion.
4. Take the self-assessment on page 5.

First Discussion:

Introducing our Global Village to the Cosmos

Does life exist on other planets? A spacecraft will be launched into deep space to find out. What would you place on board the spacecraft to communicate the diversity of Earth's culture? In this discussion, you will make a list of the items your group would send.

Messenger to Distant Worlds

Is there life on other planets? If there is intelligent life on other planets, what message would you send them? In 1977, the U.S. space program, NASA, sent a spacecraft on a one-way journey to outer space. The spacecraft was named Voyager. Part of Voyager's mission was to carry items that would communicate to aliens the richness and diversity of life on the planet Earth. Now, the United Nations is planning another spacecraft in the Voyager series, Earth Ambassador I. Your team has been called upon to decide what to send that best represents the diversity of life on Earth. As with any spacecraft, size and weight are limited. In your selections, be specific.

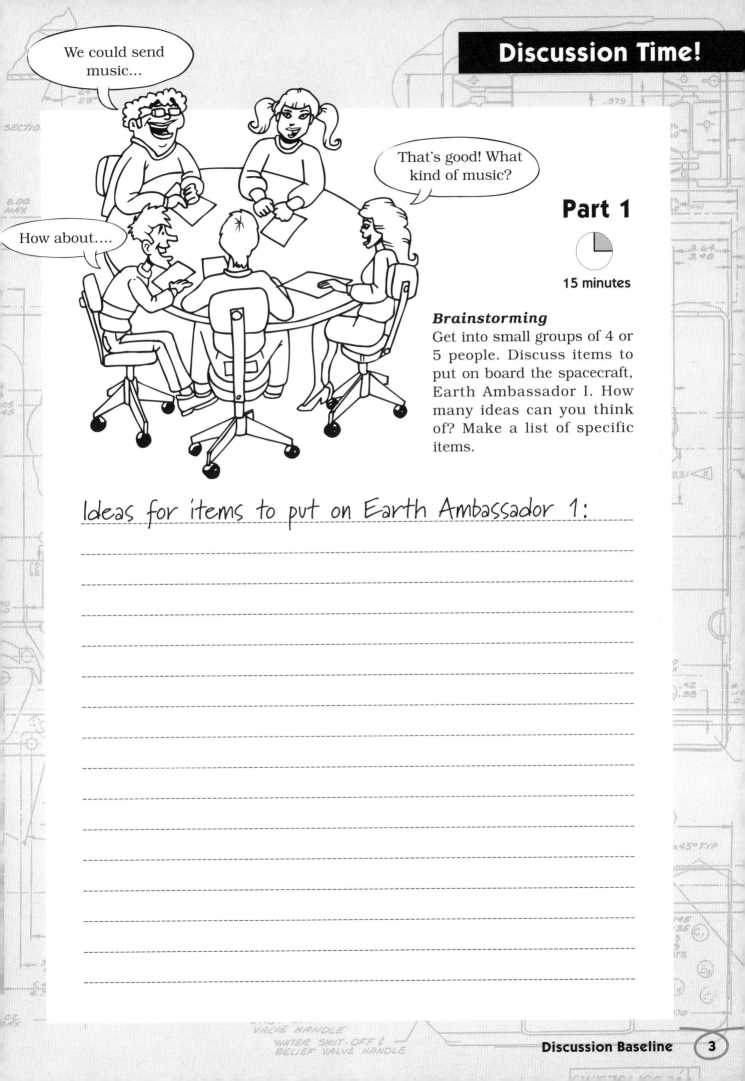

Part 1

15 minutes

Brainstorming
Get into small groups of 4 or 5 people. Discuss items to put on board the spacecraft, Earth Ambassador I. How many ideas can you think of? Make a list of specific items.

Ideas for items to put on Earth Ambassador 1:

Part 2

15 minutes

Process of Elimination

Now continue your discussion. Space and weight are very limited in the cargo area. From your list, your group can select only five items to go on board. Which ones will you select? Why?

Our Final Five Items:

Finished? Now do the self-assessment on the next page. 👉

◆ **How did you do?**

Congratulations! You have finished your first discussion. How do you feel about your performance in this discussion? Did you have a good time? How do you feel about your group's performance? Was it a good experience for everyone? Check your individual performance and your group's performance by taking this self-assessment quiz.

◆ **Group Assessment**

Group Assessment

1. How active was your group?
   a. All group members participated about equally.
   b. Some of the members did most of the talking.
   c. One person did most of the talking.
   d. We were silent much of the time.

2. Did your group encourage quiet, shy members to participate?
   a. There were no quiet or shy members in our group.
   b. Yes, we did
   c. No, we didn't
   d. I didn't notice.

3. How many items did your group come up with in Part 1, Brainstorming?
   a. 15 or more.
   b. 10 to 15.
   c. 5 to 10.
   d. less than 5

4. How many questions did your group ask each other?
   a. More than 10
   b. Between 5 and 10
   c. Between 1-5
   d. 0

5. Did your group finish the discussion within the time limit?
   a. Yes.
   b. We needed more time for Part 1 of the discussion.
   c. We needed more time for Part 2 of the discussion.
   d. We needed more time for both parts of the discussion.

Self Assessment

♦ *Individual Assessment*

Individual Assessment

1. How active were you?
   a. I did OK. I am satisfied with my participation.
   b. I should have talked less and listened more.
   c. I should have talked more.
   d. I was embarrassed by my English and didn't participate.

2. Did you encourage quiet, shy members to participate?
   a. There were no quiet or shy members in our group.
   b. Yes, I did.
   c. No, I didn't.
   d. I was a quiet, shy group member.

3. How many items did you suggest in Part 1, Brainstorming?
   a. I suggested 6 or more items
   b. I suggested three to five items.
   c. I suggested one or two items.
   d. None.

4. In this discussion, how many questions did you ask?
   a. More than 8
   b. Between 3 and 8
   c. 1 or 2
   d. 0

5. Did you take any notes during the discussion?
   a. I wrote down my ideas and everyone else's.
   b. I wrote down some ideas.
   c. I wrote down a few ideas.
   d. I didn't take any notes.

Now turn to page 124 for your Self-Assessment Scoring

STAGE ONE

Discussion as Sharing

Discussion
Process
Stage 1

♦ *Discussion as Sharing*

Discussion is a process that includes sharing, exploring. and decision making. In part one of the discussion process, we look at sharing our experiences, and our ideas.

Sharing Your Experiences:

We can learn from each other by sharing our experiences, our stories.

Sharing Your Ideas:

**Everyone freely tosses out ideas, the serious and the silly.
Everyone lays their cards on the table.**

Sharing Your Experiences

Discussion Loop 1 ◆ *Sharing Your Experiences*

Sharing our experience is the simplest and most fundamental type of discussion. We are defined by our experiences. We are shaped by our experiences. When we share our experiences, we are sharing our personal truth.

Discussion Principle 1 ◆ *Respect Every Voice—Be a Good Listener*

When sharing experiences, the group learns to value and appreciate diversity. To appreciate diversity, a participant must become a good listener.

Discussion Topic ◆ *Sharing Our Good Times and Our Bad Times*

What do we all have in common? We have all had good times. We have all had bad times. Share yours with the group.

Discussion Dynamics

Discussion Lab 1.1 ◆ *Discussion Dynamics*

What do you bring to the table? What can you contribute to your discussion group? Everyone has something to contribute to a discussion. Everyone brings something different and useful to the table. However, there seems to be an optimum, or best size, for a discussion group. In the following discussion activity, let's find out how many heads are better than one!

Round 1 ◆ *Pairs*

Work with a partner. Look at the collection of items on the following page. Which of these items do you have with you right now? Check off the items that you or your partner have. Count the items and write that number on the clipboard under Round 1 Result.

I've got a stapler and a highlight marker. What have you got?

Tell your partner what you have. Ask your partner what they have.

I've got a pencil.

Round 2 ◆ *Groups of Four*

Work with another pair. Now, as a group of four, find out what additional items your new partners bring to the table. How many more items can you check off? Mark the clipboard under Round 2 Result.

We have a Stapler and a Pencil.

We have a ruler and a cellphon

Round 3 ◆ *Larger Groups*

Form groups of 6 to 8. Find out what additional items your new partners bring to the table. How many more items can you check off? Mark the clipboard.

Does anybody have a rubber band?

Who's got an eraser?

We still need a ...

Discussion Dynamics

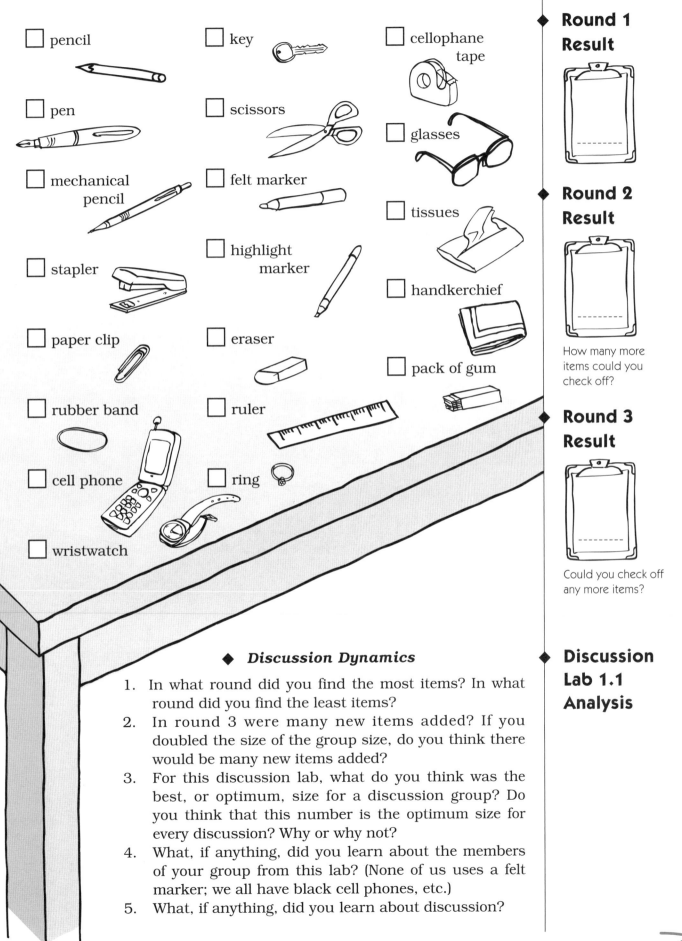

☐ pencil

☐ pen

☐ mechanical pencil

☐ stapler

☐ paper clip

☐ rubber band

☐ cell phone

☐ wristwatch

☐ key

☐ scissors

☐ felt marker

☐ highlight marker

☐ eraser

☐ ruler

☐ ring

☐ cellophane tape

☐ glasses

☐ tissues

☐ handkerchief

☐ pack of gum

◆ **Round 1 Result**

◆ **Round 2 Result**

How many more items could you check off?

◆ **Round 3 Result**

Could you check off any more items?

◆ **Discussion Lab 1.1 Analysis**

◆ *Discussion Dynamics*

1. In what round did you find the most items? In what round did you find the least items?
2. In round 3 were many new items added? If you doubled the size of the group size, do you think there would be many new items added?
3. For this discussion lab, what do you think was the best, or optimum, size for a discussion group? Do you think that this number is the optimum size for every discussion? Why or why not?
4. What, if anything, did you learn about the members of your group from this lab? (None of us uses a felt marker; we all have black cell phones, etc.)
5. What, if anything, did you learn about discussion?

Diversity of Experience

Discussion Lab 1.2 ◆ ***Diversity of Experience***

"What do you bring to the table?" doesn't mean things that you actually bring. It really means your experiences. In this lab we measure your group's collective experience, or diversity of experience.

It's a Small World ◆ ***Your Travel Experiences***

Where have you been in the world? Make small groups. Each group should have the same number of members. Where have you been? Find out the travel experiences of your group. Write the names of the countries your group has visited on the card on the next page.

◆ Diversity of Experience

1. How many countries has your group been to? The group with the most countries has the greatest diversity of experience.
2. Look at the list of countries. Have several people been to the same place? What countries would your group be best at answering questions about?

◆ **Discussion**
Lab 1.2
Analysis

Discussion Lab 1.3 ◆ *Depth of Experience*

Visiting a country for a few days and living there for several years are different levels of experience. In addition, there is a significant difference between the experiences of a 5-year old child and a 25 year-old adult.

Interview ◆ *Overseas Experiences*

In this lab, we measure the depth of experience in your group. Interview each other about where you have been, when you were there, and how long you stayed. Fill out the form on the next page.

Depth of Experience

Name _____

What country did you visit?	When were you there?	How long did you stay?

Name _____

What country did you visit?	When were you there?	How long did you stay?

Name _____

What country did you visit?	When were you there?	How long did you stay?

Name _____

What country did you visit?	When were you there?	How long did you stay?

◆ **Discussion Lab 1.3 Analysis**

◆ *Depth of Experience*
1. Look at your group's depth of experience. What countries would your group be best at answering questions about? Is your answer the same or different from your answer to question number 2 in the Discussion Lab 1.2 Analysis? Why or why not?
2. Which do you think is more important for discussions, diversity of experience or depth of experience?

✳ Respect Every Voice ✳

Be a good listener

Discussion Principle #1

◆ *Respect Every Voice ~ Be a Good Listener*

Most people think of discussion as people talking. But in a discussion group of 5 people how much time does each person spend talking? How much time does each person spend listening? Probably each person only spends 20% of the time talking and 80% of the time listening. Being a good listener is even more important than being a good speaker!

Listening 1

Audio CD Track 02

◆ *Attitudes and Actions*

Your attitudes are reflected in your actions. Look at the actions in the picture. Listen to the attitudes on the CD. Match the voices with the people below. The first one is done for you.

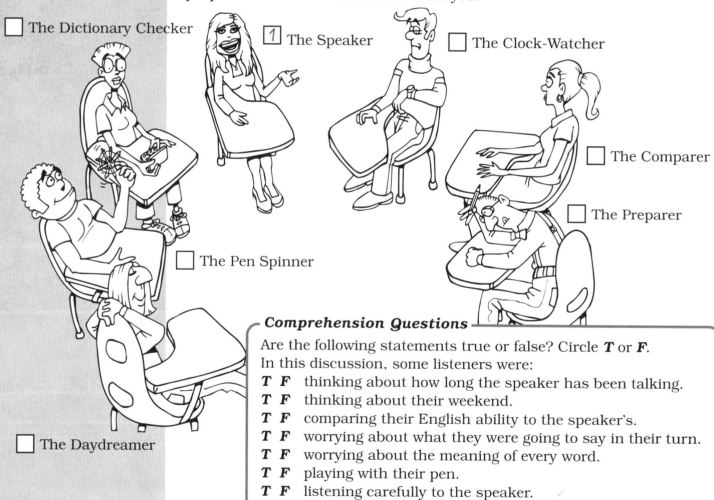

☐ The Dictionary Checker

1 The Speaker

☐ The Clock-Watcher

☐ The Comparer

☐ The Preparer

☐ The Pen Spinner

☐ The Daydreamer

Comprehension Questions

Are the following statements true or false? Circle **T** or **F**.
In this discussion, some listeners were:

T F thinking about how long the speaker has been talking.
T F thinking about their weekend.
T F comparing their English ability to the speaker's.
T F worrying about what they were going to say in their turn.
T F worrying about the meaning of every word.
T F playing with their pen.
T F listening carefully to the speaker.

Discussion Principle Questions

◆ *Discussion Principle Questions*

1. Do you think the listeners had a good attitude toward the speaker?
2. Have you ever been a Clock-watcher, a Daydreamer, a Comparer, a Dictionary Checker, a Pen Spinner, or a Preparer?

◆ *Better Attitudes, Better Actions*

Look at the picture below. Listen to the voices on the CD. Do you notice any difference in their attitudes and actions?

◆ **Listening 2**
Audio CD Track 03

┌─ **Comprehension Questions** ─────────────────────

Are the following statements true or false? Circle **T** or **F**.
In this discussion, the listeners were:

T F   listening to the speaker instead of thinking about the weekend.
T F   looking for good points about what the speaker was saying.
T F   listening without judging the speaker.
T F   giving the speaker all their attention.
T F   looking for similarities instead of differences.
T F   listening carefully to the speaker.

└──

◆ *Discussion Principle Questions*

1. What is different between the two discussions? What are the differences in their body language, their actions? What are the differences in their thoughts, their attitudes?

2. What do you think listeners need to do when the speaker is sharing their experience? In other words, what kind of behavior should the listeners practice in this discussion loop?

◆ **Discussion Principle Questions**

Discussion Phrase Bank

Study the five functions of this Discussion Loop. Use these phrases, attitudes, and actions when sharing your experiences and showing respect for every voice.

INTRODUCING YOUR EXPERIENCE

◆ *Introducing your Experience*

( ) Let me tell you about one of my best experiences...

( ) Let me tell you about one of my worst experiences...

( ) One of my best experiences was when...

( ) One of my worst experiences was when...

( ) I remember when...

( ) There was this time I was...

DETAILS OF YOUR EXPERIENCE

◆ *Giving Details of your Experience*

(Who was it with?)

> *"It was with a taxi driver"*

(Where was it?)

> *"It was in New York."*

(When was it?)

> *About 6 months ago I took a taxi...*

(What happened?)

> *I was able to answer all his questions.*

(Why was this one of your best experiences?)

> *I felt good about my English ability.*

FOCUS ON THE SPEAKER

◆ Make eye contact

Nod your head

O.K. I want to hear what she has to say...

LISTEN NON-JUDGMENTALY

◆

LOOK FOR SIMILARITIES

◆

Me too! I have done the same thing.

The Discussion:

Sharing Our Good Times and Our Bad Times

What do all of us have in common? We have all had good times. We have all had bad times. In this discussion, you will share one of your best experiences and one of your worst experiences with your classmates.

Sharing Our Stories

It is the first day of class! It is time to get to know your classmates. How can you best get to know them? By learning their names? How much do you really know about a person when you learn their name or where they are from? We learn what a person is really like from their experiences, from their stories. When you share successful experiences, you inspire others to believe in success. When you share difficult experiences, you inspire others to overcome difficulty. In this discussion, you are going to share one of your best and one of your worst experiences with your classmates.

Model Discussion ◆ *Sharing Your Experience*

In this discussion, you will be sharing one of your best experiences and one of your worst experiences. In the following model, you will hear one student sharing one of her best language learning experiences and one of her worst language learning experiences.

Listening 1 ◆ *Best Experience*

Audio CD Track 04

Listen to this student's story about one of her best experiences. Take notes and answer the questions.

1. *Who was her experience with?*
2. *Where was it?*
3. *When was it?*
4. *What happened?*
5. *In summary, what was one of her best experiences?*
6. *Why was this one of her best experiences?*

Listening 2 ◆ *Worst Experience*

Audio CD Track 05

Now, listen to this student's story about one of her worst experiences. Take notes and answer the questions.

1. *Who was her experience with?*
2. *Where was it?*
3. *When was it?*
4. *What happened?*
5. *In summary, what was one of her worst experiences?*
6. *Why was this one of her worst experiences?*

◆ *Sharing one of YOUR Experiences*

Now it is your turn. Think about your experiences. Tell us a story about one of your best experiences.

◆ *Consider these Questions*

What was one of your best experiences?

Where was it?

Who was it with?

When was it?

Why was this one of your best experiences?

What happened?

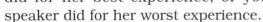

◆ *Show and Tell*

In the Model Discussion, the speaker used pictures to help her tell her stories. It is much easier to tell a story if you have something to show people. In fact, we even call it *show and tell*. Draw a rough sketch of your experience. You can draw various objects and small pictures to illustrate your story as the speaker did for her best experience, or you can draw a scene as the speaker did for her worst experience.

Discussion Loop 1 ◆ *Sharing Your Experiences*

This loop is your discussion guide. The five functions of Loop 1 will help you to share your best and worst experiences and to be a good listener.

Me too!

I have done the same thing.

LOOK FOR SIMILARITIES

Let me tell you about one of my best experiences...

INTRODUCING YOUR EXPERIENCE

O.K. I want to hear what she has to say...

About 6 months ago...

DETAILS OF YOUR EXPERIENCE

LISTEN NON-JUDGMENTALY

FOCUS ON THE SPEAKER

Discussion Challenge
How many different phrases can you use from the Discussion Phrase Bank on page 18.

Small Group Discussion ◆ *It's Your Turn!*

Get into small groups of 4 or 5 people and tell your stories. Use the pictures that you drew to help explain your best experience and your worst experience. Have fun sharing!

Option 1 ◆ *Mix It Up*

Make new groups and share your experiences again.

Sharing Your Ideas

Discussion Loop 2   ◆ *Sharing Your Ideas*

In the last Loop, we focused on sharing your *experiences*. In this unit we focus on sharing your *ideas*. Ideas are based on experiences. We all have different experiences, so we all can come up with different ideas. Coming up with ideas in a group is called *brainstorming*.

Discussion Principle 2   ◆ *Celebrate all ideas*

When sharing ideas, the group learns how to reach for synergy. To create synergy, every participant should welcome and celebrate each idea.

Discussion Topic   ◆ *Thinking Globally, Acting Locally*

A killer tsunami wrecks havoc through parts of Asia. How can your group help?"

The Synergy Factor

Discussion Lab 2.1

◆ *The Synergy Factor*

In the last unit, we saw that each participant brings something different to the table. When the total of everything on the table adds up to something even greater than the sum of what the participants bring, we call this synergy. In this lab, we will attempt to experience some synergy.

Here is a box. What could you imagine it to be?

Add a handle and it could be a coffee cup.

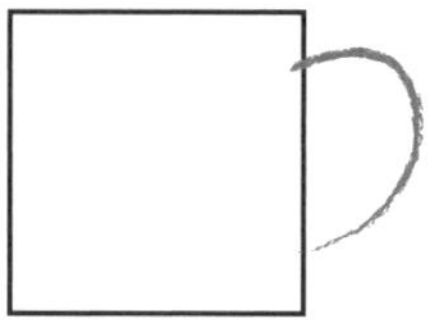

Add some ribbon and it could be a present.

Round 1

◆ *Thinking on Your Own*

Now, how many other ideas can you imagine? Here are some more boxes. What can you imagine them to be? In one minute, sketch as many ideas as you can.

> The number of ideas is important, not the quality of your drawing!

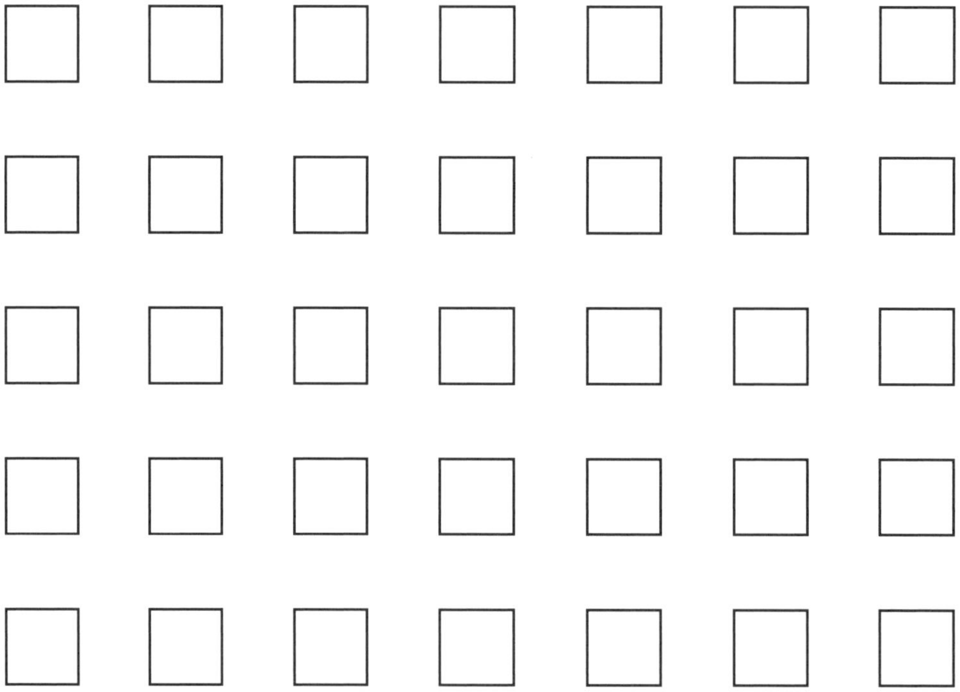

◆ *Brainstorming in a Group*

Now, form groups of 3 to 5 people. As a group, brainstorm more ideas for the boxes. Try to let one idea lead to the next. In other words, use one idea as a springboard for the next idea. Sketch the new ideas that your group comes up with.

◆ **Round 2**

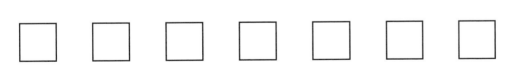

Sketch *ONLY* the new ideas that your group brainstorms here:

[ ] [ ] [ ] [ ] [ ] [ ] [ ]

[ ] [ ] [ ] [ ] [ ] [ ] [ ]

[ ] [ ] [ ] [ ] [ ] [ ] [ ]

[ ] [ ] [ ] [ ] [ ] [ ] [ ]

◆ *Reaching for Synergy*

1. How many ideas did you think of by yourself?
2. Did the other members of your group have the same ideas or different ideas?
3. How many new ideas did your group think of in your brainstorming session, 3 ideas? 5 ideas? 8 ideas? More?
4. Do you feel that your group experienced synergy in this Lab? Why or why not?

◆ **Discussion**
Lab 2.1
Analysis

Brainstorming

Discussion Lab 2.2 ◆ *Brainstorming*

Coming up with many ideas quickly in a group is called brainstorming. There are no mistakes or incorrect answers when brainstorming. We do not judge or criticize the ideas. We just try to create as many possibilities as we can. There are many ways to brainstorm in a group. Here are four techniques to try.

| *Verbal Brainstorming* | *Vertical Brainstorming* | *Horizontal Brainstorming* | *Mapping* |

Round 1 ◆ *Verbal Brainstorming*

The first brainstorming technique is called *verbal brainstorming*, or thinking out loud. By listening to each other freely tossing out ideas you can come up with even more ideas. In 60 seconds name as many colors as you can. Shout out the colors!

Red!

Blue!

Green!

● *Could you brainstorm continuously for 1 minute or did you run out of ideas?*

◆ *The Vertical Brainstorming Technique*

Another brainstorming technique is called *vertical brainstorming*, or listing. By listing ideas on the whiteboard or a piece of paper, you can see your ideas and come up with more ideas.

◆ *Vertical Brainstorming - Cities -*

In 2 minutes, list as many cities as you can. Choose one person to write. Shout out the cites! Write them down.

◆ **Round 2**

◆ **Now You Try It!**

Vertical Brainstorming: Cities

Don't worry about the spelling!

❶ *How many cites could your group brainstorm?*

❷ *Which group brainstormed the most cities?*

Brainstorming

Round 3 ◆ *The Horizontal Brainstorming Technique*

The next brainstorming technique is called, *horizontal brainstorming*, or following a line of thought. Here is an example.

The first line of thought is capital cities. The next line of thought is cities in near the sea. The next line of thought is cities in Europe. Can you guess what the next line of thought is?

Now You ◆ *Horizontal Brainstorming - Animals -*
Try It!

Choose a new person to write. On the whiteboard or on a piece of paper use horizontal brainstorming to list as many animals as you can in 2 minutes. Make sure to tell your group members your line of thought.

❶ *How many animals could your group brainstorm?*

❷ *Which group brainstormed the most animals?*

Discussion as Sharing

◆ *The Mapping Technique*

The final brainstorming technique is called *mapping*. Here is an example.

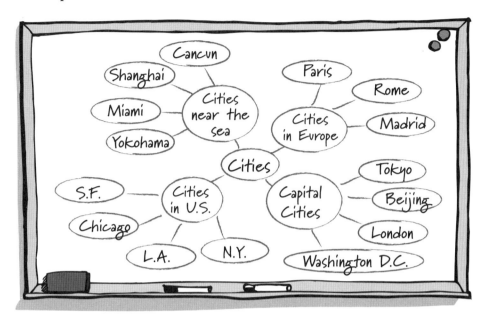

The cities are grouped around different themes or areas. For example, capital cites, cities in the United States, cities in Europe, cities near the sea.

◆ *Mapping - Countries -*

Choose another person to write. On the whiteboard or on a piece of paper use mapping to brainstorm as many countries as you can in 3 minutes.

❶ *How many countries could your group brainstorm?*

❷ *Which group brainstormed the most countries?*

◆ *Brainstorming*

In this lab, you used four brainstorming techniques, verbal, vertical, horizontal, and mapping. Which one did you like best? Why?

◆ **Round 4**

◆ **Now You Try It!**

◆ **Discussion Lab 2.2 Analysis**

✳ Celebrate All Ideas ✳

Be an active and supportive participant

Discussion Principle #2

◆ *Celebrate All Ideas—Be an Active and Supportive Participant*

In a brainstorming session, the group needs to create a supportive environment. Everyone must contribute ideas, encourage ideas, and expand on the ideas. Welcome all ideas, silly and serious! Synergy can turn silly ideas into great ideas!

Listening 1

Audio CD Track 06

◆ *Silence is NOT Golden*

Listen to these students discussing their global issues project. Answer the questions below.

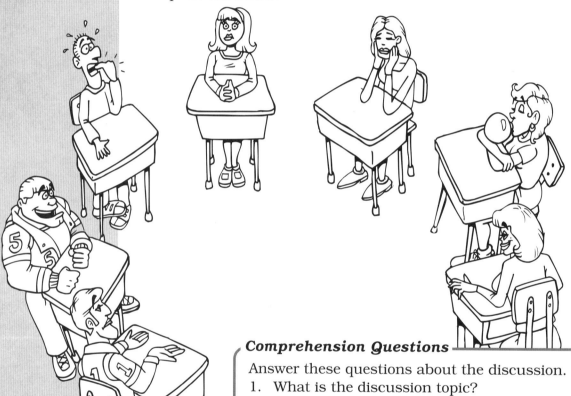

Comprehension Questions

Answer these questions about the discussion.
1. What is the discussion topic?
2. How many participants were there?
3. How many ideas were contributed?

Discussion Principle Questions

◆ *Discussion Principle Questions*

1. Would you want to be in this group?
2. Do you feel this group had synergy?
3. How would you feel if you were this discussion leader?
4. Do you think this group will be successful in brainstorming a lot of ideas?
5. How could this group improve their brainstorming?
6. Have you ever been in a discussion group that acted like the group above?

◆ *Celebrating Ideas*

Listen to what happens when a group celebrates all ideas. When every member of the group is an active participant, the synergy inspires the group to generate more and greater ideas. Listen to these students discussing their global issues project and answer the questions below

◆ **Listening 2**
Audio CD Track 07

Comprehension Questions

Answer these questions about the discussion.
1. How many participants were there in this group?
2. How many ideas were contributed this time?
3. What was the first idea? How was it expanded?

◆ *Discussion Principle Questions*

1. What is different in this discussion?
2. Would you want to be in this group?
3. Do you feel this group had synergy?
4. Do you think this group will be successful in brainstorming a lot of ideas?
5. Have you ever been in a discussion group that acted like this group?

◆ **Discussion Principle Questions**

Discussion Phrase Bank

Study the three functions of this Discussion Loop. Use these phrases to share your ideas and be an active and supportive participant. How many phrases can you use in your discussion?

CONTRIBUTE IDEAS

◆ *Contribute*

( ) How about ...

( ) Maybe a....

( ) You could...

( ) What about this:....

( ) What if we...

ENCOURAGE IDEAS

◆ *Encourage*

( ) Good idea!

( ) Yeah, yeah, yeah!

( ) I like that!

( ) Yeah, way to go!!

( ) Wow!

( ) Sounds good!

( ) Yeah, that's brilliant.

( ) Good thinking!

EXPAND ON IDEAS

◆ *Expand*

( ) That gives me an idea...

( ) And another idea would be

( ) Yeah, and we could also...

( ) Yeah! And...

The Discussion:

Thinking Globally, Acting Locally.

A killer tsunami wrecks havoc through parts of Asia. When a disaster strikes how can your class help? In this discussion, you will brainstorm ideas to help the tsunami victims.

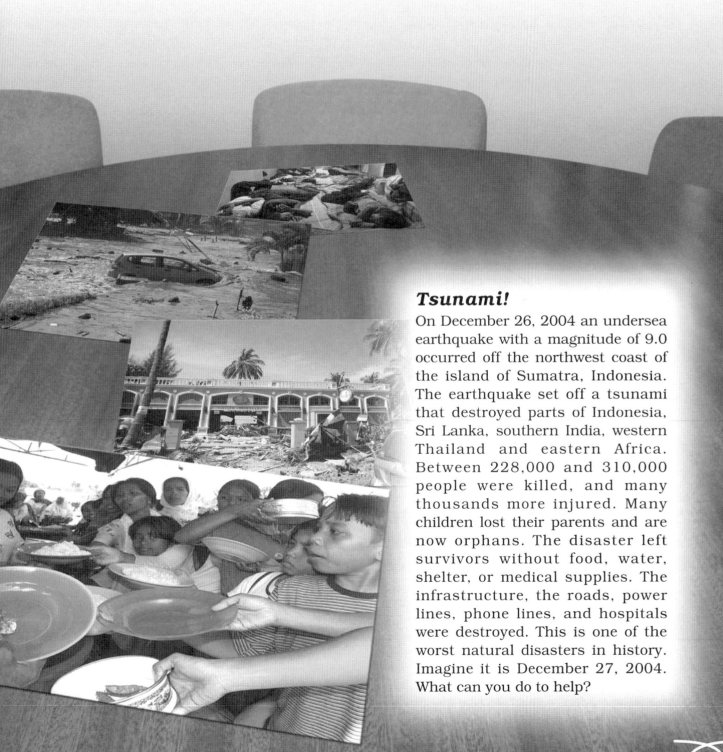

Tsunami!

On December 26, 2004 an undersea earthquake with a magnitude of 9.0 occurred off the northwest coast of the island of Sumatra, Indonesia. The earthquake set off a tsunami that destroyed parts of Indonesia, Sri Lanka, southern India, western Thailand and eastern Africa. Between 228,000 and 310,000 people were killed, and many thousands more injured. Many children lost their parents and are now orphans. The disaster left survivors without food, water, shelter, or medical supplies. The infrastructure, the roads, power lines, phone lines, and hospitals were destroyed. This is one of the worst natural disasters in history. Imagine it is December 27, 2004. What can you do to help?

Model Discussion: How Can We Help?

Model Discussion

◆ *Sharing Your Ideas*

In this discussion, you, as college students, will be brainstorming ways to help the victims and survivors of the December 2004 Tsunami.

Listening

Audio CD Track 08

◆ *What Can We Do To Help?*

Listen to this group in action. Working in groups of three, record the ideas you hear. One person should record the ideas using vertical brainstorming, the second person records the ideas using horizontal brainstorming, and the third person records the ideas using the mapping technique. Suggested starting points are written on the whiteboards below.

Vertical Brainstorming Technique

Horizontal Brainstorming Technique

Mapping Brainstorming Technique

Compare

◆ *Which Brainstorming Technique did you Prefer?*

Now compare. Did everyone have the same ideas? Which brainstorming technique was easy? Which was most useful?

◆ *What are YOUR Ideas for Helping the Tsunami Victims?*

Now it is your turn! Think about your experiences helping others. Use your experiences to help you come up with ideas for your discussion.

◆ **Prepare For Your Discussion**

◆ *Your Experience Helping Others*

What experience do you have helping others? Check the boxes.

Experience Checklist

	Yes	No
1. Have you had any experience raising money for charity?	❏	❏
2. Do you know anyone who has?	❏	❏
3. Have you ever raised money for your club at school?	❏	❏
4. Have you ever read about someone who raised money for charity?	❏	❏
5. Have you ever seen a charity event on television?	❏	❏
6. Have you ever been a volunteer?	❏	❏
7. Do you know anyone who has done volunteer work?	❏	❏

◆ *Consider these Questions*

Before beginning your discussion consider these questions.

When are we going to do it?

Who is going to do it?

Where are we going to do this?

What exactly are we going to do?

How are we going to do it?

Discussion Loop 2 ◆ *Sharing Your Ideas*

This loop is your discussion guide. The three functions of Loop 2 will help you to brainstorm and share your ideas to help the tsunami victims.

Discussion Challenge
How many different phrases can you use from the Discussion Phrase Bank on page 34.

Small Group Discussion ◆ *Brainstorm Ideas to Help the Tsunami Victims.*

Now it is your group's turn! Get into small groups and brainstorm ideas to help the tsunami victims. Use one of the brainstorming techniques you have learned. Write your group's ideas on the white board below. Think of as many ideas as you can. Be specific. Be sure you can answer the Who, What, When, Where, and How for your ideas.

Continue on a separate sheet of paper if you need more space.

When everyone has competed this discussion task, turn the page and let's continue the discussion.

Option 1 ◆ *Share Your Ideas*

Share with the class or members from another group:
1. How many ideas did your group brainstorm?
2. What brainstorming technique did your group use?
3. What was the strangest idea your group came up with?
4. What was your group's best idea?

Option 2 ◆ *Best in Class*

Each group writes their 3 best ideas on the board and the class votes on the best idea.

Option 3 ◆ *Poster Presentation: How We Can Help.*

Each group selects one of their ideas and makes a poster and presents it to the class.

STAGE TWO

Discussion as Exploring

Discussion Process Stage 2 ◆ In Discussion Process Stage 1, brainstorming generated many ideas. In Stage 2, Discussion as Exploring, members of the group choose some of those ideas for further exploration. We call this taking a position. Then, the group carefully explores, or maps the position.

Mapping a position requires asking questions, clarifying, and confirming. From that, we can begin searching for the best position.

Exploring Positions

Discussion Loop 3 ◆ *Exploring Positions*

Discussion enters this loop when a participant states a belief, or a position. The group carefully explores the position, or clarifies the position. In a sense, the group is *mapping* the position. What exactly is the position? What is the extent of the position? What are the reasons for this position?

Discussion Principle 3 ◆ *Seek First to Understand*

Before agreeing or disagreeing with a position, participants must first understand it. To reach understanding, participants must set aside their own positions, and first try to understand the speaker's position.

Discussion Topic ◆ *Who are Your Heroes*

Nominating inspirational people for the cover of *Hero Magazine.* Who has inspired you to believe, or to do, more than you thought possible? A new magazine wants your input.

The Orange Story

Discussion Lab 3.1

The Orange Story

Have you ever been in a dilemma, a problem that seems to have no solution? Listen as Dianne struggles with a dilemma.

Listening 1
Audio CD Track 09

The Dilemma

Listen to the Orange Story and answer the questions:

1. How does Dianne feel? Is she tired? Why?
2. What is Dianne's position, in other words, what does she want? Why?
3. What is her dilemma ?

◆ **Listening 1**
continued...

◆ *What Should She Do?*

Make small groups and discuss the following.

1. What should Dianne do? Give her some advice!
2. How many suggestions can your group brainstorm in 3 minutes?

◆ **Discussion Task 1**

Dianne should...

They ought to...

Why don't they...

The Orange Story

Listening 2

Audio CD Track 10

The Question

The Orange Story continues. Listen and answer the questions:

1. What is different this time?
2. Why does the man need the orange?
3. What part of the orange does he need?
4. What part of the orange does Dianne want?

Discussion Task 2

A Win/Win Solution?

1. Can you see a win/win solution that would satisfy both people?
2. Is your new solution on your list of ideas from the previous page? Why not?

◆ **The Solution**

Listen to the conclusion of the Orange Story and answer these questions:

1. What is Dianne's solution?
2. Who is going to pay for the orange?

◆ **Listening 3**
Audio CD Track 11

◆ **The Whole Story**

Look at the original list of suggestions you brainstormed.

1. How many of the suggestions you originally brainstormed on page 45 were solutions?
2. How many of the suggestions were questions about the problem?
3. Do you usually ask questions before disagreeing, arguing or offering a solution?

◆ **Discussion
Lab 3.1
Analysis**

✳ Seek First To Understand ✳

Ask questions: clarify and confirm

Discussion Principle #3

◆ *Seek First to Understand*

Discussion is based on a community of respect. Mutual understanding is reached through mutual respect. If you want others to respect your position, you need first to respect their position. If you want someone else to listen to your position, you should first listen to his or her position. Don't argue. Listen! Ask questions! Understand!

Listening 1

Audio CD Track 12

◆ *Seeking First to Speak*

Listen to this group discussing the subject of their school report.

Comprehension Questions

Answer these questions about the discussion.
1. What was each person's position, who did they want to do their report on?
   1st speaker: _____ Gandhi _____
   2nd speaker: _____
   3rd speaker: _____
2. Do you know the reasons why the 1st speaker chose Gandhi?
3. Do you know the reasons for the 2nd speaker's choice?
4. Do you know the reasons for the 3rd speaker's choice?

Discussion Principle Questions

◆ *Discussion Principle Questions*

1. Do you think they understand each other's choices? Did they attempt to understand each other?
2. Was this a discussion or an argument? Why do you think so?
3. Have you ever experienced a situation like this with friends, co-workers, or family?

◆ *Seeking First to Understand*

Listen again to this group discussing the subject of their school report.

Comprehension Questions

Answer these questions about the discussion.
1. How many positions were presented in this discussion?
2. What reason did the first speaker give for recommending Gandhi?

◆ *Discussion Principle Questions*

1. By the end of the discussion, do you think everyone understood the speaker's position?
2. Do you think that the speaker was satisfied with this discussion?
3. What is the difference between the first discussion and this discussion?

◆ **Discussion Principle Questions**

Discussion Phrase Bank

Study the four functions of this Discussion Loop. Use these phrases to explore and understand positions. How many of these phrases can you use in your discussion?

TAKING A POSITION

◆ *Taking a Position*
( ) I think that...
( ) I believe that....
( ) In my opinion...
( ) My position is...
( ) I would like to...
( ) We should...

ASKING QUESTIONS

◆ *Asking Questions*
( ) Why do you need the orange?
( ) What about the inside of the orange?
( ) Who is baking a pie?
( ) When does she need the orange?
( ) Where is she baking the pie?
( ) How much of the orange does she need?

CLARIFYING A POSITION

◆ *Clarifying*
( ) What I meant was...
( ) What I imagined was...
( ) What I was trying to say...
( ) Well, I think the answer is...
( ) The reason is that...
( ) Because...

CONFIRMING A POSITION

◆ *Confirming*
( ) So, what you are saying is..
( ) So, what I'm hearing is...
( ) ...is that right?

The Discussion:

Who are Your Heroes?

Who has inspired you to believe or to do more than you thought possible? A new magazine wants your input. In this discussion, you will nominate people for the cover of *Hero Magazine.*

Our Greatest Heroes

Time magazine recently published a special issue featuring the world's 100 most influential people. In addition, each year *Time* magazine selects The Person Of The Year. *People* magazine does People Of The Year. *Forbes* magazine features The Most Influential Business people of the Year. The new magazine *Hero* is seeking nominees for the cover of their *Greatest Heroes of All Time* issue. If you were asked to nominate three people, who would they be?

Model Discussion ◆ *Exploring Positions*

Each of you will be asked to nominate three people for the *Greatest Heroes of All Time* cover. Then, in the discussion you will take turns asking each other questions about your choices. The group will consider your answers and choose one of the three to be your final nominee.

Listening ◆ *I'd Like to Nominate...*

Audio CD Track 14

Listen to this model discussion. Write down the speaker's three nominees, and the groups' final choice.

Name: Kim

Group Member 1:

Nominee 1:

Nominee 2:

Nominee 3:

Final Nominee:

◆ *Who are YOUR Heroes?*

Now it is your turn. Write your 3 nominees for *Greatest Heroes of All Time* in the spaces below. They can be famous heroes or your personal heroes. Make notes about your reasons for choosing them.

◆ **Prepare For Your Discussion**

MY NOMINEES FOR HERO MAGAZINE:

Nominee 1:

Reasons:

Nominee 2:

Reasons:

Nominee 3:

Reasons:

Discussion ◆ *Exploring Positions*
Loop 3

This loop is your discussion guide. The four functions of Loop 3 will help you explore the reasons for choosing the nominees for the cover of *Hero Magazine*.

So, what you are saying is...
...right?

CONFIRMING A POSITION

I think that...

TAKING A POSITION

What I meant was...

CLARIFYING A POSITION

Why do you think that... ?

ASKING QUESTIONS

Discussion Challenge!
How many different phrases can you use from the Discussion Phrase Bank on page 50.

Small Group Discussion ◆ *Our Nominees for the Greatest Heroes of All Time!*

Now it is your group's turn! Form small groups and discuss your nominees for the cover of *Hero Magazine*. Ask questions and narrow each person's nominees down to one final nominee. The group listens to each individual's answers about their three nominees and then the group votes to decide which of the three nominees will be the final nominee for that individual. Write each group member's name, their three nominees and the group's choice for each member's final nominee in the boxes below.

Name:

Group Member 1:

Nominee 1:

Nominee 2:

Nominee 3:

Final Nominee:

Name:

Group Member 2:

Nominee 1:

Nominee 2:

Nominee 3:

Final Nominee:

Name:

Group Member 3:

Nominee 1:

Nominee 2:

Nominee 3:

Final Nominee:

Name:

Group Member 4:

Nominee 1:

Nominee 2:

Nominee 3:

Final Nominee:

Name:

Group Member 5:

Nominee 1:

Nominee 2:

Nominee 3:

Final Nominee:

When everyone has competed this discussion task, turn the page and let's continue the discussion.

Option 1 ◆ *Announcing the Nominees*

Audio CD Track 15

Listen to this model and then try it yourself!

Group one's nominees for Hero of the Year are_____, _____, _____, and _____.
Congratulations to all nominees.
Next, please welcome from group number two _____ and _____ .

Option 2 ◆ *Final Nominees*

Each group lists all of its nominees on the board. The whole class asks each group questions about their nominees and then the class chooses one final nominee for each group.

Option 3 ◆ *Panel Discussion*

Each group selects one of its hero nominees for the panel. The heroes on the panel introduce themselves. The class asks each "hero" questions. The teacher can serve as moderator or emcee.

Option 4 ◆ *Presentation on One Nominee*

Each group researches one nominee and makes a short presentation with pictures, DVD clips, etc.

Loop 4

Searching for the Best Position

Discussion Loop 4 ◆ *Searching for the Best Position*

After the group reaches mutual understanding, it has earned the right to agree, disagree, and support each other's positions. In this loop, we enter the real *give and take* of discussion. Through this process we look for the best position.

Discussion Principle 4 ◆ *Separate People from Positions*

While looking for the best position, participants learn how to respect the person when disagreeing with the position.

Discussion Topic ◆ *The Entertainment Hall of Fame*

What movies, songs, books, and TV programs deserve special recognition? The new Entertainment Hall of Fame wants your recommendations.

Possibility, Probability, and Certainty

Discussion Lab 4.1 ◆ *Possibility, Probability, and Certainty*

Some things in life are certain, some are probable, and some are possible. This lab asks about your level of certainty.

Problem 1 ◆ *Count the Squares*

A square has 4 sides of equal length. Look at the illustration below. How many squares do you see? Count the number of squares.

Turn to page 124 to check your answer.

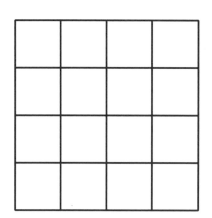

Write your answer here
Number of squares: _____

CERTAINTY CHECK

How sure are you of your answer? Check one.

100%	I'm positive.	❑
75%	I'm pretty sure.	❑
25%	I'm not really certain.	❑
0%	I'm not confident at all.	❑

Problem 2 ◆ *The Sum of the Angles...*

How many degrees in a triangle? Is this always true?

Turn to page 125 to check your answer.

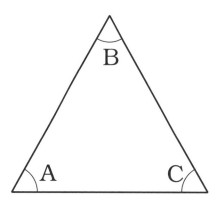

Write your answer here
$\angle A + \angle B + \angle C =$ _____
❑ Always true ❑ Not always true

CERTAINTY CHECK

How sure are you of your answer? Check one.

100%	I'm positive.	❑
75%	I'm pretty sure.	❑
25%	I'm not really certain.	❑
0%	I'm not confident at all.	❑

Discussion Lab 4.1 Analysis ◆ *Discussion Lab Analysis*

1. Were your answers correct?
2. How certain were you of the answers?
3. Certainty is a dangerous position to take. There are very few certainties in life. New information and new experiences can change your mind. Can you think of some things in life that are certain? Some things that are probable? Some things that are possible?

◆ ***Everyone Knows***

Sometimes common sense does not make sense. Listen to these examples of when common sense was wrong.

◆ **Discussion Lab 4.2**

◆ ***Everyone Knows the Earth is Flat!***

Listen to this discussion.

◆ **Listening 1**

Audio CD Track 16

❶ *Who was the story about?*

❷ *What was the reaction of the King's ministers?*

◆ ***Everyone Knows People Can't Fly!***

Listen to this discussion.

◆ **Listening 2**

Audio CD Track 17

❶ *Who was this story about?*

❷ *What was the bank manager's reaction?*

◆ ***Keep an Open Mind***

1. Keep an open mind! Be open to new ideas! Can you think of two or three other examples of people having closed minds?

◆ **Discussion Lab 4.2 Analysis**

✳ Separate People From Positions ✳

Disagree without making the speaker wrong

Discussion Principle #2

◆ *Separate People from Positions*

In this Loop, we look for the best position. As we do this, disagreement is common and even necessary. A participant should always remember to respect the person while disagreeing with the position. Compare positions, not people. Say, "I like this position better than that position." Don't say, "I like Hanna's position better than Mari's." Talk about the weak points of positions, not of the participants. Say, "This position is not logical." Don't say, "You are not logical!"

Listening 1

Audio CD Track 18

◆ *You are Wrong!*

Listen to this discussion about an advertising campaign for sports shoes. Answer the questions below:

Comprehension Questions

Answer these questions about the discussion.
1. What is Charlie's idea for the new ad campaign?
2. Who agreed with him?
3. Which of these phrases were used to show disagreement?
   a. You always come up with the strangest ideas.
   b. Your idea is really not very good.
   c. Larry's idea is much better than yours.
   d. Larry is right and you are wrong.

Discussion Principle Questions

◆ *Discussion Principle Questions*
1. Were they attacking the person or the position?
2. If you were Charlie, how would you feel?

◆ *You are Right about that, but...*

Match the phrase on the left with the phrase on the right. Note how the speaker agrees before disagreeing.

AGREEING

❶ That's an interesting idea...

❷ You are right. Young people do need more culture...

DISAGREEING

Ⓐ but don't you think that a rap artist will appeal more to young people.

Ⓑ but I don't see how an opera singer will appeal to young people.

◆ *Discussion Principle Questions*

1. This time were they attacking the person or the position?
2. Now, if you were Charlie, how would you feel?

◆ **Discussion Principle Questions**

Discussion Phrase Bank

Study the four functions of this Discussion Loop. Use these phrases to look for the best positions while keeping people and positions separate. How many of these phrases can you use in your discussion?

DISAGREEING WITH POSITIONS

◆ *Disagreeing*

( ) That certainly is one possibility but...

( ) I don't see how/why...

( ) I'm not so sure about that because...

( ) I don't think that is true in this case because...

( ) That might be true but...

( ) A lot of people might agree with that but...

EVALUATING POSITIONS

◆ *Evaluating*

( ) I agree that ____ is important. But what about ____?

( ) You are right about that. But I don't understand _____.

( ) I like ____. I don't like _____

( ) I see the point about ____ but I don't see the point about....

DEFENDING POSITIONS

◆ *Defending*

( ) Let me put it another way....

( ) I think the point I'm trying to make here is...

( ) I don't think that I am saying....

AGREEING WITH POSITIONS

◆ *Agreeing*

( ) I'd have to agree that....

( ) I think that's a good point.

The Discussion:

The Entertainment Hall of Fame.

What movies, songs, books, and TV programs deserve special recognition? The Entertainment Hall of Fame wants your recommendations! In this discussion, you will select three movies to go into the Hall of Fame.

The Hall of Fame

Have you heard of the Baseball Hall of Fame? How about the Rock and Roll Hall of Fame? Did you know that there is even a Robot Hall of Fame? A hall of fame is a museum that celebrates the best of the best. For example, The Rock and Roll Hall of Fame was founded in 1983 to celebrate the greatest musicians, songwriters, DJs, and others in the music industry. Every year the nominating committee selects between 5 to 7 people to be added to the Hall of fame. A new museum, The Entertainment Hall of Fame, is opening next year. If you were on the nominating committee, which three movies would you recommend for The Hall of Fame?

Model Discussion: Hall of Fame Nominees

Model ◆ *Searching for the Best Position*
Discussion

A new museum, The Entertainment Hall of Fame, is opening next year and you are the nominating committee. This Hall of Fame will feature the best movies of all time. Listen to this nominating committee discussing their choices. Answer the questions below.

Listening 1 ◆ *Seeking First to Understand*

Audio CD Track 20

Write Mia's three nominees for best movie in the spaces below.

Mia's Nominees:

1. _____

2. _____

3. _____

Listening 2 ◆ *Disagreeing with Positions*

Audio CD Track 21

Listen to Al, Mia, and Eddie, and answer the questions below.

1. What is Al's position? In other words, what movie does he think should be in the Entertainment Hall of Fame?
2. How does Mia respond? What movie does she think would be better?
3. How does Al defend his position?
4. How does Mia evaluate that position? What part did she agree with? What part did she disagree with?
5. Who does Eddie agree with and why?

◆ *Reaching Agreement*

Listen and cross out the movies the group eliminates. Circle the group's third nominee.

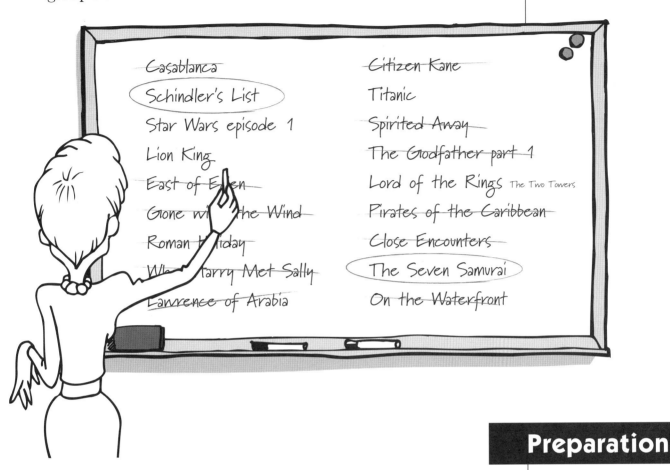

Casablanca
Schindler's List
Star Wars episode 1
Lion King
East of Eden
Gone with the Wind
Roman Holiday
When Harry Met Sally
Lawrence of Arabia

Citizen Kane
Titanic
Spirited Away
The Godfather part 1
Lord of the Rings The Two Towers
Pirates of the Caribbean
Close Encounters
The Seven Samurai
On the Waterfront

◆ *What do YOU Think are the 3 Greatest Movies of All Time?*

Now it's your turn. Write your 3 nominees for the greatest movies of all time on the cards below. Make notes about your reasons for choosing them.

MY NOMINEES:

Nominee 1:	Nominee 2:	Nominee 3:
Reason:	Reason:	Reason:

Discussion ◆ Searching for the Best Position
Loop 4

This loop is your discussion guide. The four functions of this loop will help you in your search for the 3 greatest movies of all time.

Discussion Challenge!
How many different phrases can you use from the Discussion Phrase Bank on page 62.

Small Group ◆ *Our Nominees for the Three Greatest Movies of All Time.*
Discussion   Now it is your group's turn to discuss nominees for the
                     Entertainment Hall of Fame!

Step 1 ◆ *Our Nominees*
             In small groups, write everyone's nominees on the whiteboard
             below. Feel free to ask each other questions about the movies
             nominated.

Our Nominees for the 3 Greatest Movies of All Time

Continue on a separate sheet of paper if you need more space.

Step 2 ◆ *Our Finalists*
             Discuss until your group can agree on three movies to nominate for
             inclusion in the Entertainment Hall of Fame. Write those three
             movies in the boxes below.

1. _____   2. _____   3. _____

When everyone has competed this discussion task, turn the page and let's continue the discussion.

Option 1 ◆ *Share Your Results*

Each group puts their nominees on the board and class chooses the best three.

Option 2 ◆ *Nominate 3 Musicians*

Each group nominates three singers or bands for the Entertainment Hall of Fame.

Option 3 ◆ *Nominate 3 Books*

Each group nominates three books for the Entertainment Hall of Fame.

Option 4 ◆ *Nominate 3 Television Shows*

Each group nominates three TV shows for the Entertainment Hall of Fame.

Discussion as Decision Making

Thinking Inside and Outside the Box

In Part 3, the discussion process leads to making a decision. In Loop 5, the decision making process begins with thinking about what a solution might look like. In other words, we build a box that defines the problem, and then, in loop 6, we look for solutions that might fit the box. Finally, in loop 7, we choose the best solution.

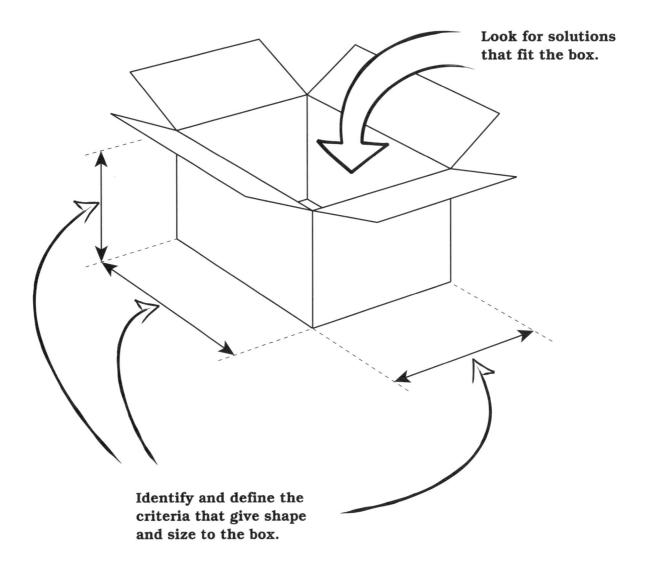

Look for solutions that fit the box.

Identify and define the criteria that give shape and size to the box.

Identifying the Criteria

Discussion Loop 5 ◆ *Identifying the Criteria*

In this loop, we take the first step in problem solving. A problem is like an empty box. The solution to a problem is what we can find to fit within that box. The best fit is the best solution. The requirements or specifications for this fit are called the criteria. Therefore, in this loop, the criteria we identify will be used to build and define that empty box.

Discussion Principle 5 ◆ *Know Your Criteria*

To build a box that is satisfactory to all participants, the group must find the key criteria or requirements for all members.

Discussion Topic ◆ *Finding the Right Person for the Right Job*

What are your values? What are your needs? Can you find a company that matches your values and needs? Do you match theirs?

Identify Your Criteria

◆ *Identify Your Criteria*

How do you make decisions? What factors, or criteria, do you consider? For example, if you are looking for a partner, a boyfriend or a girlfriend, what do you look for? What is important to you? Age? Appearance? Education? When making a decision we begin by identifying the criteria.

Step 1 ◆ *Which Criteria do I Think are Important?*

What do you look for in a partner? Check the characteristics, the criteria, that you think are important in choosing a partner.

❏ *Age*	❏ *Body Shape*	❏ *Hair Style*	❏ *Car*
❏ *Height*	❏ *Voice*	❏ *Income/Money*	❏ *Weight*
❏ *Job*	❏ *Health*	❏ *Blood Type*	❏ *Cleanliness*
❏ *Personality*	❏ *Nationality*	❏ *Birth Order*	❏ *Sense of Humor*
❏ *Religion*	❏ *Hobbies*	❏ *Intelligence*	❏ *Face/Looks*
❏ *Education*	❏ *Fashion Sense*	❏ *Race*	❏ *Smoker*

Step 2 ◆ *I Think the Five Most Important Characteristics in a Partner are...*

Now write the 5 that you think are most important in the spaces below:

♥ _____ ♥ _____ ♥ _____ ♥ _____ ♥ _____

◆ *What Would a Solution Look Like?*

1. Compare your 5 criteria with a partner? How many did you have in common?
2. We use tables similar to this everyday to make decisions. In this case, the horizontal axis, along the top, lists your criteria for choosing a partner. What do you think goes down the other axis?

◆ *Define Your Criteria*

Now that you have identified the criteria, do you really understand the criteria? For example, if age is the criterion, how old is too old? How young is too young? What range of ages is acceptable to you? The criteria we each consider may be similar but everyone is different and everyone has a different range of what is acceptable within that criteria.

◆ **Discussion Lab 5.2**

◆ Interview a classmate. Find out their criteria for an ideal partner from Discussion Lab 5.1. Write their 5 criteria next to the hearts below.

◆ **Step 1**

◆ Now, continue your interview. Ask your classmate to define their criteria with numbers and examples. Write them in the white boxes below the hearts.

◆ **Step 2**

For age, he should be between 19 and 22.

For personality, I like someone with a good sense of humor. For example, I like someone who enjoys comedies.

◆ *Define the Criteria*

1. Which criteria were easy to define? Which criteria were difficult to define?
2. Some criteria can be measured. We can define them with numbers. We call these *objective* criteria. Were some of your criteria objective? Which ones?
3. Other criteria can't be defined by numbers. We define these by giving examples. We call these *subjective* criteria. Were some of your criteria subjective? Which ones?

◆ **Discussion Lab 5.2 Analysis**

✳ **Know All Your Criteria** ✳

Know what you want, get what you need

Discussion Principle #5

◆ *If you Know What you Want, you can get What you Need.*

The box you build now determines what the solutions will look like. Think carefully about your own criteria. Find out the criteria of the other group members. Otherwise, the solution you find might not be acceptable to you or others in the group. Know all your criteria to make better decisions.

Listening 1

Audio CD Track 23

◆ *The Only Criterion*

Listen to the husband shop for shoes for his wife. Answer the questions below.

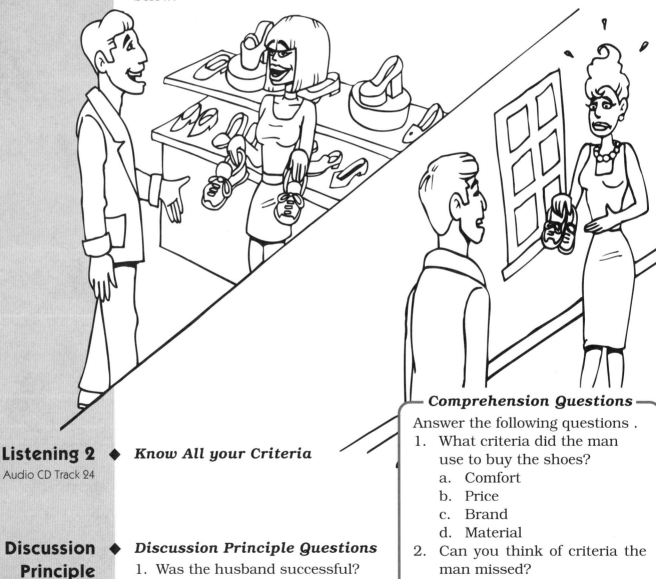

Listening 2

Audio CD Track 24

◆ *Know All your Criteria*

┌─ *Comprehension Questions* ─┐
Answer the following questions .
1. What criteria did the man use to buy the shoes?
   a. Comfort
   b. Price
   c. Brand
   d. Material
2. Can you think of criteria the man missed?

Discussion Principle Questions

◆ *Discussion Principle Questions*
1. Was the husband successful?
2. Why or why not?

♦ **Identify your Criteria**

What were the criteria? Can you fill in the chart below?

Style	Size	Color	Price	Heel
Formal				

♦ **Listening 3**
Audio CD Track 25

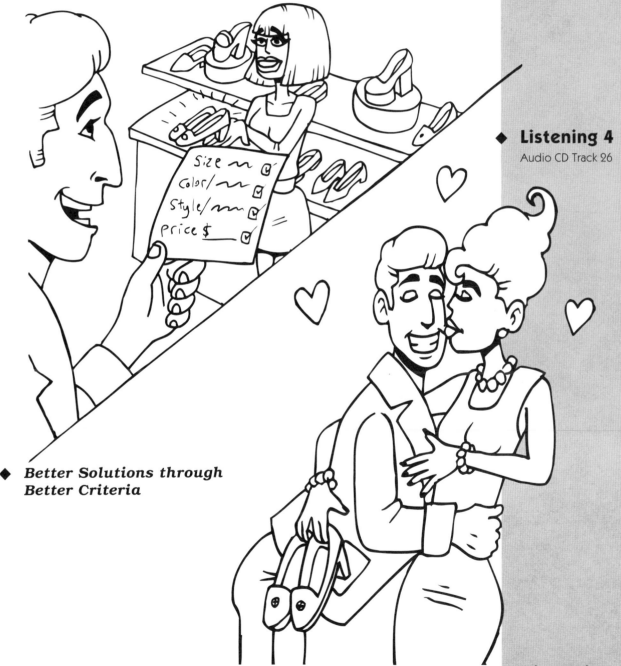

♦ **Listening 4**
Audio CD Track 26

♦ **Better Solutions through Better Criteria**

♦ **Discussion Principle Questions**

1. Was the husband successful this time?
2. Why or why not?

♦ **Discussion Principle Questions**

Discussion Phrase Bank

Study the three functions of this Discussion Loop. Use these phrases to identify, narrow, and define the criteria. How many of these phrases can you use in your discussion?

IDENTIFYING THE CRITERIA

◆ *Brainstorming Positive Criteria*
( ) They have to be black, formal shoes.
( ) They ought to have at least a two-inch heel.
( ) They need to be a size 7.
( ) They've got to be...
( ) They should have...

◆ *Brainstorming Negative Criteria*
( ) They can't have rubber soles.
( ) They shouldn't be too expensive.

NARROWING THE CRITERIA

◆ *The Process of Elimination*
( ) I don't think price is so important.
( ) I think price is more important than color.
( ) Isn't price more important than color?

DEFINING THE CRITERIA

◆ *Defining Objective Criteria*
( ) It needs to be between $75 and $100.
( ) No more than $100.
( ) No less than 2 inches.
( ) At least 2 inches
( ) At most $100.

◆ *Defining Subjective Criteria*
( ) For example, a style like in this picture.
( ) Just like the color of my old shoes.
( ) Similar to the ones we saw last week

The Discussion:

Finding the Right Person for the Right Job

What are your values? What are your needs? Can you find a company that is your match? In this discussion, you will identify criteria from two points of view, the employer and the employee.

Job and Career Fairs

Many universities and high schools sponsor job fairs or career fairs where employers can find employees, and employees can find employers. In other words, companies can find workers, and students can find jobs. For a company, finding the right employees is a constant challenge. For a student, finding the right job is one of the most important decisions in their life. In this discussion you will prepare for a job fair. First, you will think about what is important to the employer, then you will think about what is important to the job seeker.

Model Discussion ◆ *Identifying the Criteria*

In this discussion, you will prepare for a job fair interview. Listen to these students discussing the upcoming job fair. Your discussion should follow the same stages as theirs.

Listening 1 ◆ *Identifying the Criteria*

Audio CD Track 27

Listen. What two criteria did they mention? Write them in the boxes below.

Criteria 1:	Criteria 2:	

Listening 2 ◆ *Narrowing the Criteria*

Audio CD Track 28

Listen. What criterion did they eliminate? Cross out the box above.

Model Discussion

◆ ***Defining the Criteria***

Listen. What question did they think of? Write it below.

Listening 3
Audio CD Track 29

◆ ***Considering Both Sides***

Listen. One side of the issue is the employer's criteria for employees. What is the other side of the issue? Write it below.

Listening 4
Audio CD Track 30

Preparation

◆ ***What do THEY want? What do YOU want?***

Now it is your turn. Think about both sides of the issue. Fill in the table below. Make notes from the employer's point of view, and from your point of view.

Prepare for Your Discussion

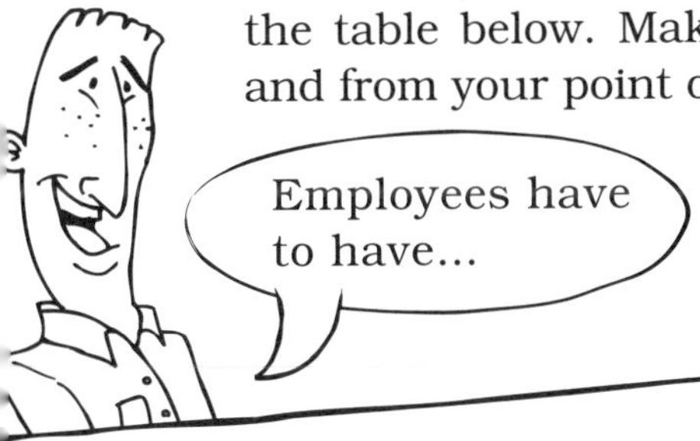

Employees have to have...

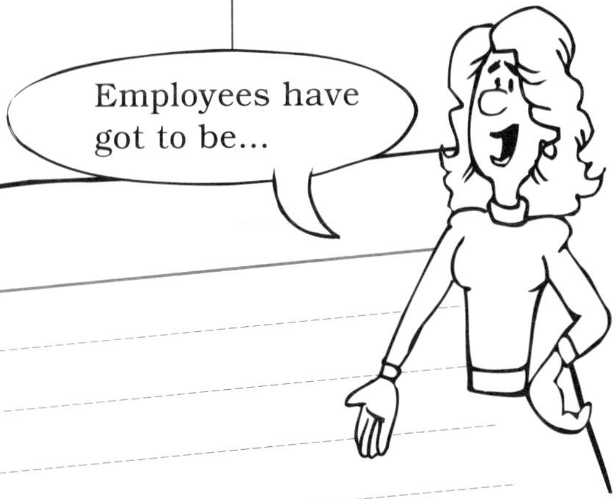

Employees have got to be...

What employers want in an employee:

What employees want in a job:

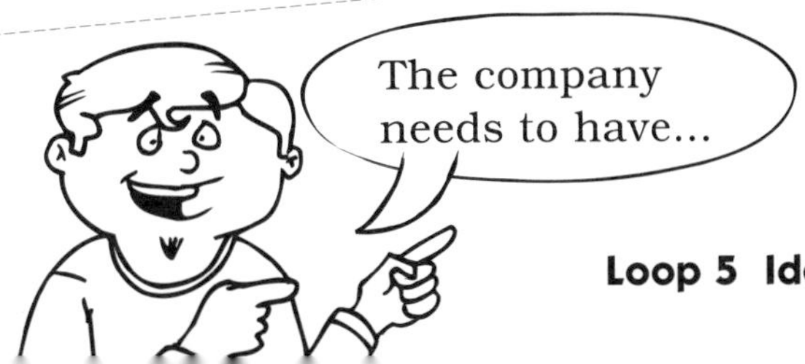

The company needs to have...

Discussion Time!

This loop is your discussion guide. The three functions of the criteria loop will help you identify what both employers and employees are looking for.

Employees need to be between... and...

Employees have to be...

DEFINING OBJECTIVE CRITERIA

BRAINSTORMING POSITIVE CRITERIA

DEFINING THE CRITERIA

For example...

IDENTIFYING THE CRITERIA

Employees shouldn't be...

DEFINING SUBJECTIVE CRITERIA

I don't think that is so important.

BRAINSTORMING NEGATIVE CRITERIA

NARROWING THE CRITERIA

Discussion Challenge
How many different phrases can you use from the Discussion Phrase Bank on page 76.

Employer's Point of View

◆ *What Employers Really Want*

Now it is your group's turn to discuss what a company really looks for in an employee. Form small groups. Imagine that you are a company hiring new employees. Follow the steps below.

Step 1 ◆ *Identify the Criteria*

From an employers' point of view, brainstorm criteria for hiring new employees.

Step 2 ◆ *Narrow the Criteria*

Choose the top 5 criteria and enter below.

Criteria 1:	Criteria 2:	Criteria 3:	Criteria 4:	Criteria 5:
_____	_____	_____	_____	_____

Step 3 ◆ *Define the Criteria*

To help you define the criteria, imagine specific questions an employer would ask about each of the criteria.

Questions about criteria 1:

Questions about criteria 2:

Questions about criteria 3:

Questions about criteria 4:

Questions about criteria 5:

Step 4 ◆ *Share your Results*

Now compare your criteria with other groups. Are your criteria similar? Are they different? How many criteria do you have in common?

Employee's Point of View ◆ ***What Employees Really Want***

Now it is your group's turn to discuss what job seekers look for in an employer. Form small groups and follow the steps below.

Step 1 ◆ ***Identify the Criteria***

From an employee's point of view, brainstorm criteria for choosing a company to work for.

Step 2 ◆ ***Narrow the Criteria***

Choose the top 5 criteria and enter below.

Criteria 1:	Criteria 2:	Criteria 3:	Criteria 4:	Criteria 5:

Step 3 ◆ ***Define the Criteria***

To help you define the criteria, imagine specific questions you would like to ask the employer.

Questions about criteria 1:

Questions about criteria 2:

Questions about criteria 3:

Questions about criteria 4:

Questions about criteria 5:

Step 4 ◆ ***Share your Results***

Now compare your criteria with other groups. Are your criteria similar? Are they different? How many criteria do you have in common?

◆ *The Job Interview*

In the previous two small group discussions, you identified and defined criteria from both the employers' point of view and the employees' point of view. This experience is good preparation for a job interview. Listen to this job interview and complete the chart. One of the applicants is well prepared the other is not. What questions did the interviewer ask? What answers did each of the job seekers give? What questions did each job applicants ask?

◆ **Listening**
Audio CD Track 31

Questions	Job Applicant 1	Job Applicant 2

Job Applicant 1 Questions	Job Applicant 2 Questions

● Which applicant do you think will get the job? Why?

When everyone has competed this discussion task, turn the page and let's continue the discussion. ☞

Let's Continue the Discussion

Option 1 ◆ *Job Fair*

Let's practice attending a job fair. Hold a job fair with interviews.

Step 1

Return to your original discussion groups. Half of each group will take the role of employers looking for employees, the other half will be students looking for jobs.

Step 2

Employers set up company booths around the room.

Step 3

Job seekers move from booth to booth interviewing for jobs. In your interviews, use the criteria and questions from your small group discussions.

Listing the Options

Discussion Loop 6 ◆ *Listing the Options*

In the last Loop, we focused on building the box by identifying and defining the criteria. In this Loop, we list possible solutions, possible options, that fit our criteria and thus fit our box.

Discussion Principle 6 ◆ *Uncover your Assumptions*

Sometimes the best options, the best solutions do not seem to fit inside the box. To look outside the box, each participant must examine their assumptions, and be willing to discard them. We call this ability *thinking outside the box.*

Discussion Topic ◆ *Designing a Menu for the International Palate*

The planning committee for the International Student Welcome Party must come up with a single menu for students from 5 continents.

Discussion ◆ *Thinking Outside the Box*
Lab 6.1
In the last unit we focused on building the box by identifying and defining the criteria. In this lab we will explore thinking outside the box.

The 9-Dot ◆ *Connect the Dots*
Puzzle
Can you connect these nine dots using only 4 straight lines, and without lifting your pencil from the paper? Work together in small groups. You have 3 minutes.

Discussion ◆ *Could you Do it?*
Lab 6.1
Analysis
1. Could you connect the dots?
2. Are you thinking inside the box or outside the box? What if you could extend the lines beyond the square formed by the nine dots?
3. Try again. Now could you connect the dots? If not, see page 125.

Discussion ◆ *Assumptions*
Lab 6.2
To think outside the box, you need to find your assumptions. An assumption is something that you think is true but is not necessarily true. In this lab we will try to uncover our assumptions.

The Orchard ◆ *Plant the Orchards*
Puzzle
Get into small groups. Imagine that you are farmers. You are planting an apple orchard, a pear orchard and a cherry orchard.
- Each orchard has a different set of criteria.
- Plant the orchards to satisfy the criteria given in the Planting Instructions.
- These are the only criteria.
The apple orchard is already planted for you.

Apple Orchard Planting Instructions

Number of trees: **9**

Number of rows: **3**

Number of trees per row: **3**

The Apple Orchard

Pear Orchard Planting Instructions

Number of trees: **12**

Number of rows: **4**

Number of trees per row: **3**

The Pear Orchard

Cherry Orchard Planting Instructions

Number of trees: **10**

Number of rows: **5**

Number of trees per row: **4**

The Cherry Orchard

◆ *What's Stopping You?*

1. Could you plant all of the orchards? Which one was difficult?
2. Are you assuming the trees need to be planted in parallel rows? Was that one of the criteria?
3. Are you assuming the trees need to be evenly spaced? Was that one of the criteria?
4. Try again. Now could you plant all the orchards? If not, see page 125.

◆ **Discussion Lab 6.2 Analysis**

Multi-Dimensional Thinking

Discussion Lab 6.3

♦ *Multi-Dimensional Thinking*

Another way of thinking outside the box is to explore different directions or different dimensions. Don't limit yourself to one or even two dimensions. Become a multi-dimensional thinker! Be creative! Increase your options!

The 4-Square Puzzle

♦ *Arrange the Squares*

Here are 4 squares of paper. You must arrange them on the grid so that each square touches no more than two other squares. How many different configurations can you think of?

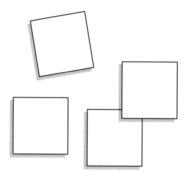

Work in small groups. How many options can your group think of? Tell your partners where to place the squares. Record your group's configurations (options) on the following page.

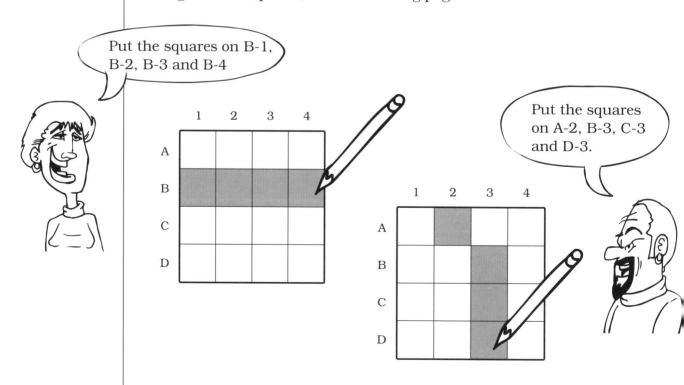

Put the squares on B-1, B-2, B-3 and B-4

Put the squares on A-2, B-3, C-3 and D-3.

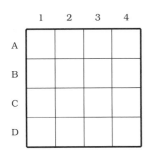
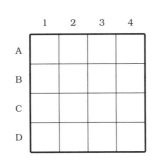
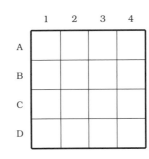
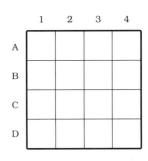

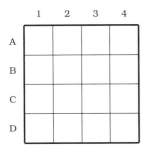
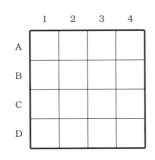
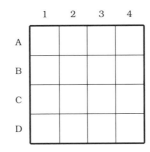
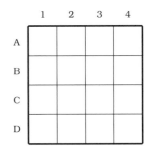

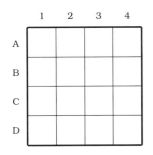
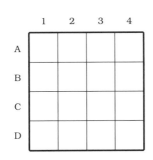
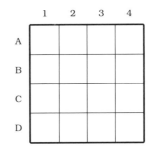
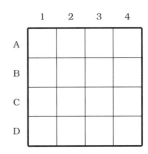

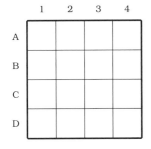
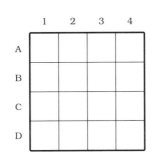
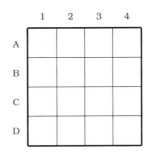
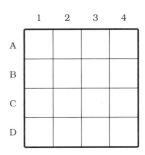

Discussion
Lab 6.3
Analysis

◆ *How many Dimensions did you Think in?*

1. How many configurations (options) did your group think of?
2. Which configuration was the most creative?
3. Did you think of any 3-dimensional configurations?
   If not, see page 125.

✳ Uncover Your Assumptions ✳

Find your assumptions, multiply your options

Discussion Principle #6

◆ *Find Your Assumptions—And go Beyond Them*

To think outside the box, we redefine the box by challenging its dimensions/specifications. In other words, we find our assumptions and make the box bigger or different. Increase the number of options, by challenging your assumptions!

Listening 1

Audio CD Track 32

◆ *Thinking Inside the Box*

Listen to these students planning their school picnic. Answer the questions below.

--- **Comprehension Questions** ---

1. How many options did they think of?
2. Why were coffee and tea rejected?

Discussion Principle Questions

◆ *Discussion Principle Questions*

1. What is this group assuming?
2. Can you think outside of the box and find a solution?

◆ *Thinking Outside the Box*

Now listen to the same students planning the school picnic. See what happens when they find their assumptions and go beyond them.

◆ **Listening 2**
Audio CD Track 33

── **Comprehension Question** ──
How many options did they think of now?

◆ *Discussion Principle Questions*

1. What assumption did they uncover?
2. In the days of Christopher Columbus, what assumption did many people make?

◆ **Discussion Principle Questions**

91

Discussion Phrase Bank

Study the four functions of this Discussion Loop. Use these phrases to list options and uncover your assumptions. How many phrases can you use in your discussion?

SUGGESTING OPTIONS

◆ *Suggesting*

( )   Would this be OK?

( )   Would this work?

( )   Would this fit our criteria?

( )   Would this fit?

( )   What if we did this?

REJECTING OPTIONS

◆ *Rejecting*

( )   I don't think that would work because...

( )   But that doesn't fit our criterion of...

LOOKING FOR ASSUMPTIONS

◆ *Looking for Assumptions*

( )   Does it have to be hot?

( )   What are we assuming here?

( )   We are assuming that...

( )   Are we assuming that...?

( )   Is it really necessary that...?

( )   Do we really have to...?

( )   What would happen if we...?

ACCEPTING OPTIONS

◆ *Accepting*

( )   That would work!

( )   That might be good!

( )   That's perfect!

( )   That's a possibility!

The Discussion:

Designing a Menu for the International Palate

What would you serve to a multi-national, multi-cultural group of students? The planning committee for the International Student Welcoming Party must come up with a single menu for students from 5 continents. In this discussion, you will need to design a menu that satisfies everyone.

A Welcoming Party

Does your school have an international exchange program for foreign students? How does your school welcome them? Eating a meal together is a universal human ritual. One of the great joys in life is learning about other cultures through food. What we eat helps define who we are. Food reflects our culture, diet, and even our religion. If you had to plan a menu for a party of international students, what would you serve? Imagine that your class is hosting the International Student Welcoming Party. There will be students from over 30 different countries, including India, South Africa, China, Korea, Indonesia, Iran, Brazil, Canada, and Australia. Your job is to plan the menu. The menu should feature your country's food, but be satisfying to everyone at the party. Bon Appétit!

Model Discussion ◆ *Discussion Model*

In this discussion, you will plan a menu for the International Students' Welcoming Party. Listen to this group identify criteria for the menu (the **criteria loop**), and suggest various dishes (the **option loop**).

Listening 1 ◆ *Criteria Loop:*

Audio CD Track 34

What two criteria did the group mention? Write them in the boxes below.

Criteria 1:	Criteria 2:	

Listening 2 ◆ *Option Loop:*

Audio CD Track 35

Listen to the group suggest options and fill in the blanks below.

1. What food was suggested?

   They suggested serving _____.

2. Why was it initially rejected?

   Because it is too _____.

3. What was the assumption?

   They were assuming that it was a _____ lobster.

4. What solution did they find outside the box?

   They decided to serve the lobster in a _____.

◆ *What Food would YOU serve?*

Now it is your turn. Take a few minutes to think about the menu for an International Students' Welcoming Party.

◆ *YOUR own Gastronomic Experience*

What foods from other countries have you tried? Were there some foods that you liked? Some you didn't like? Why? Are there any foods that you can't eat? Are there any foods from your own country that you don't like. Make notes below.

◆ **Prepare For Your Discussion**

◆ **Step 1**

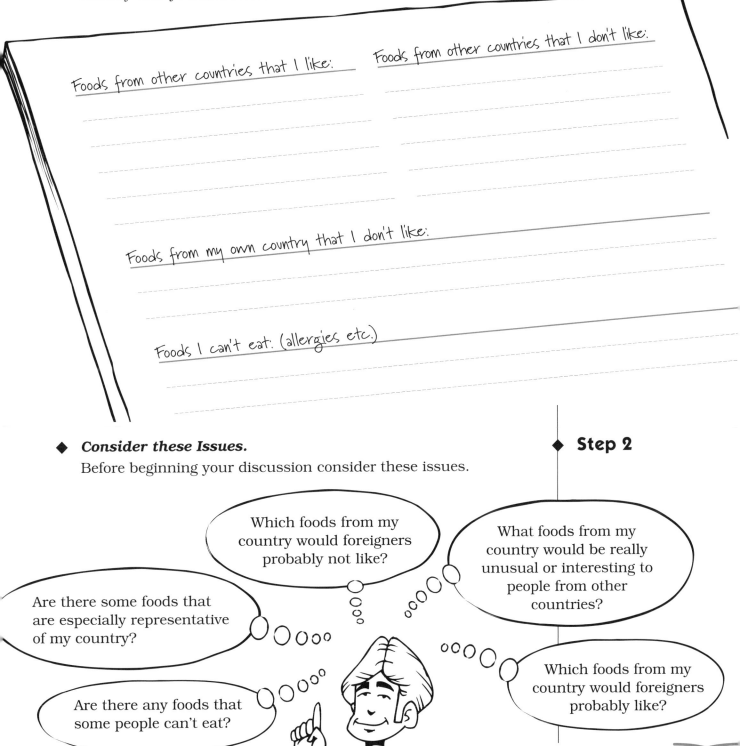

Foods from other countries that I like:

Foods from other countries that I don't like:

Foods from my own country that I don't like:

Foods I can't eat: (allergies etc.)

◆ *Consider these Issues.*

Before beginning your discussion consider these issues.

◆ **Step 2**

Which foods from my country would foreigners probably not like?

What foods from my country would be really unusual or interesting to people from other countries?

Are there some foods that are especially representative of my country?

Which foods from my country would foreigners probably like?

Are there any foods that some people can't eat?

Discussion Time!

This loop is your discussion guide. The four functions of Loop 6 will help you list the options for your International Student Menu.

That could work!

Would this be OK?
We could...

**ACCEPTING
AN OPTION**

**SUGGESTING
OPTIONS**

Does it have to be... ?

I don't think that
would work because...

**LOOKING FOR
ASSUMPTIONS**

**REJECTING
AN OPTION**

Discussion Challenge
How many different phrases can you use
from the Discussion Phrase Bank on page 92.

◆ *Criteria Loop*

Just as you did in the discussion in Loop 5, in this discussion you will have to first brainstorm and identify your criteria. Then narrow your criteria to those that you think are the most important and define those criteria. Write your criteria on a sheet of paper.

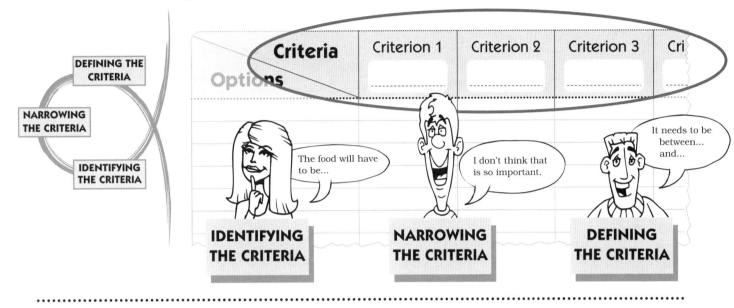

◆ *Option Loop*

After you have identified your criteria, brainstorm and suggest options that fit the criteria. Analyze the options, accepting the options that best fit the criteria and rejecting those options that do not. Be sure to look for your assumptions so that you can consider all of the options.

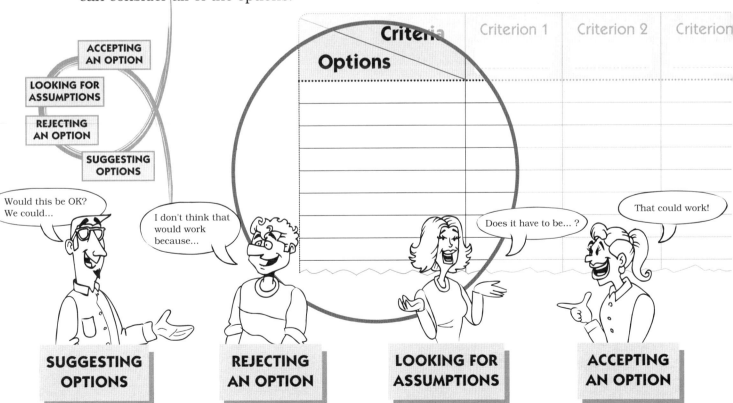

When everyone has competed this discussion task, turn the page and let's continue the discussion.

Option 1 ◆ *Make a Menu.*

Make a paper menu describing your dishes. Then make new groups composed of members from other groups and explain your menus.

Our Menu

Write your menu here.

Option 2 ◆ *What is that?*

Do you know what Palak Paneer is? Do you know what goes into Haggis? Would you want to eat Croque Monsieur? Probably your guests won't know what some of your dishes are? Help them by making menu cards like the example here. Each member of the group makes a card for one or two items from your menu.

Agedashidofu

Thick cubes of deep fried tofu bean curd served in a sauce of fish stock and soy sauce. Topped with grated ginger and shaved bonito fish flakes.

Option 3 ◆ *International Food Fair*

Have an International Food Fair. Put the menus on posters on the wall and walk around the room and decide where you would like to eat.

Choosing the Best Solution

Discussion Loop 7	◆	*Choosing the Best Solution*
		The group enters this discussion Loop when it asks, "Which is the best option?" Usually a problem will have several good solutions. How do we choose the best option, the best solution?

Discussion Principle 7	◆	*Look To Your Values*
		Sometimes the best decision is not always the easiest decision. To reach the best decision, each participant must decide first what they value most.

Discussion Topic	◆	*Studying Abroad — Where to Go and Why*
		A year of study abroad is a once in a lifetime opportunity but in which country do you spend it? A rich country? A developing country? An Asian country? An English-speaking country? How do you decide?"

Discussion ◆ *Easy Decisions*
Lab 7.1

Aloha! You and your friends are planning a vacation to Hawaii. You are deciding where to stay. You have narrowed the options down to the following 4 resorts; The Eastin, The Bilton, The Two Seasons, and the Holiday out.

In groups of four, compare information and make your final decision. Each member of the group should choose a hotel to represent. Write your name next to your hotel and turn to the page given. The other members of your group will ask you questions about that hotel.

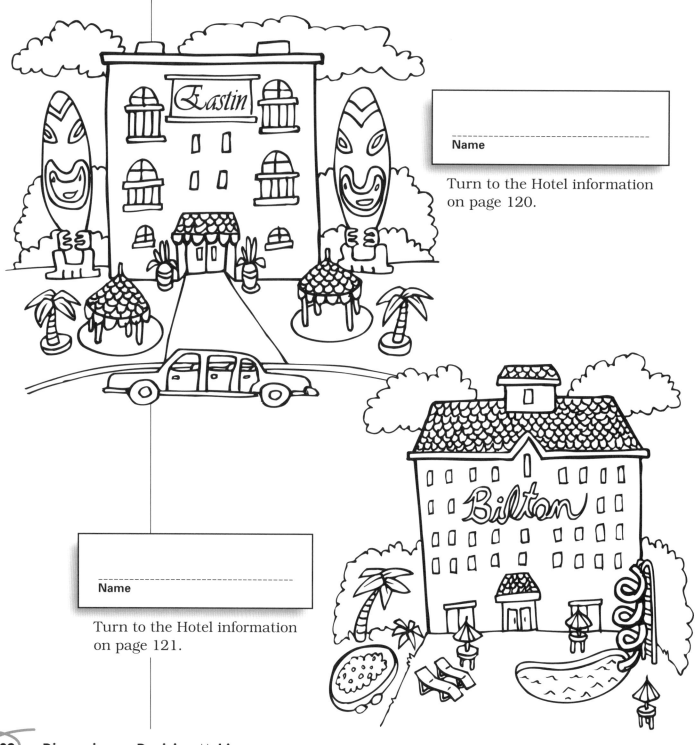

Name

Turn to the Hotel information on page 120.

Name

Turn to the Hotel information on page 121.

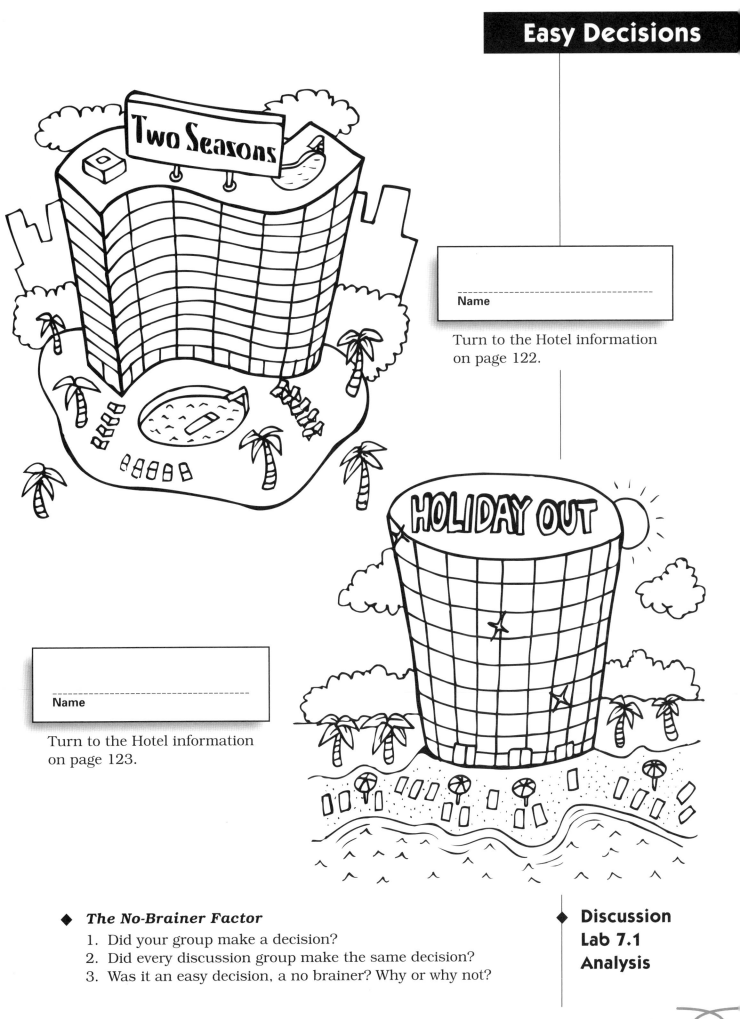

Two Seasons

HOLIDAY OUT

Name

Turn to the Hotel information on page 122.

Name

Turn to the Hotel information on page 123.

◆ *The No-Brainer Factor*

1. Did your group make a decision?
2. Did every discussion group make the same decision?
3. Was it an easy decision, a no brainer? Why or why not?

◆ **Discussion**
Lab 7.1
Analysis

Difficult Decisions

◆ *Difficult Decisions*

Consider Jamaica.... Study the table below. Decide which one your group is going to stay at. Discuss with your group and decide which Jamaican resort you prefer.

	Price	
The Bob Marley Bilton	$132 all- inclusive package	
THE REGGAE REGENCY	$207 all-inclusive package	
The Holiday Rasta Man	$205 all-inclusive package	
The Yamon Excelsior	$212 all-inclusive package	

Room	Recreational Activities	Food and Dining	Service Rating	Location
400 sq. ft. pool-side room	Swimming Golf Tennis	Features the famous Bob Marley Restaurant and Grill	5 Palm Tree Rating 🌴🌴🌴🌴🌴	Overlooking the beautiful white sands and blue waters of Montego Bay
410 sq. ft luxurious ocean view room	Scuba diving Swimming Para-sailing Horseback riding Golf Tennis Reggae lessons	Two Restaurants: The Italian Espresso Food and Drink Trattoria; The Jamaican Steak House	5 Palm Tree Rating 🌴🌴🌴🌴🌴	On scenic Montego bay
400 sq. ft. mini-suite	Swimming; Golf and tennis	7 gourmet restaurants, including the world famous five star Matsumoto Sushi and Crab House. All meals, snacks, and unlimited drinks, included. Everyday is a party at the Rasta Man!	5 Palm Tree Rating 🌴🌴🌴🌴🌴	Montego Bay, Jamaica
600 sq. ft. beach-front deluxe suite; private whirlpool bath; free in-room movies	Swimming; Golf and tennis	90 minute show with all you can eat buffet	5 Palm Tree Rating 🌴🌴🌴🌴🌴	On beautiful and historic Montego Bay

◆ *All Things Being Equal Factor*
1. Did your group make a decision?
2. Did every discussion group make the same decision? Why or why not?
3. Was it as easy as in the first lab?
4. To make a decision, did you have to assign more weight or value to some of the criteria?

◆ **Discussion Lab 7.2 Result**

✳ **Look To Your Values** ✳

Make decisions based on what you value most

Discussion Principle #7

◆ *Look To Your Values*

Decisions are based on values, and values are often based on experience. Examine your criteria. What criterion do you value most, time or money? Quantity or quality? Speed or luxury? Experience or ability? To reach the best decision, first decide what you value most.

Listening 1

Audio CD Track 36

◆ *What am I going to do?*

Listen to Charles describing his dilemma. Answer the questions.
1. What is Charles' dilemma, what does he need to decide?
2. Look at Charles' reasons in the table below. Check whether it is a reason to go or a reason to stay. The first one is done for you.

Reasons to go back to the US		Reasons to stay in Japan
☐	Have a really good job back home.	☐
☐	Don't even know what work I would do if I stayed here.	☐
☐	Supposed to get a promotion soon.	☐
☐	Just bought a new condo.	☐
☐	All my furniture is in The United States	☐
☐	All my stuff is there.	☐
☐	Don't have a place to live in Japan.	☐
☐	Nobuko.	☐

3. What is his decision and why?

Discussion Principle Questions

◆ *Discussion Principle Questions*
1. Do you think he made the right decision?
2. Why or why not?

◆ *Look to your Values*

Listen as Charles makes a decision. Answer the questions below.
1. What is his decision now?
2. What does he value most, what was his decision based on?

◆ *Discussion Principle Questions*
1. Do you think he made the right decision now?
2. Why or why not?

Discussion Phrase Bank

Study the functions of this Discussion Loop. Use these phrases as you choose the best solution based on what you value most. How many phrases can you use in your discussion?

REVIEWING THE OPTIONS

◆ *Restating the options*

( ) This one has...

( ) The advantages of this option are...

( ) The disadvantage of this one is...

( ) One good thing about this one is...

( ) The biggest drawback of this option is...

◆ *Comparing the options*

( ) This one has more ____ than that one

( ) This one has better ____ than that one

( ) The ____ is ____er than the others

( ) This one has the biggest...

WEIGHING THE CRITERIA

◆ *Prioritizing criteria*

( ) What is more important to you, ____ or ____ ?

( ) What do you value more?

( ) What criterion is most important to you?

( ) Which is the least important?

( ) Which do you think is more important ____ , or ____ ?

◆ *Stating values*

( ) To me, ____ is more important than ____ .

( ) To me, that doesn't matter.

( ) To me, that is really important.

The Discussion:

Studying Abroad — Where to Go and Why

A year of study abroad is a once in a lifetime opportunity but in which country do you spend it? A rich country? A developing country? An Asian country? An English-speaking country? How do you decide? In this discussion, your group will choose where it should go for its year abroad.

Year Abroad Programs

A year abroad is a once in a lifetime opportunity. It is a chance to experience other cultures firsthand. It is a chance to use your foreign language skills. You could do a home stay in a rich developed country to improve your language skills or you could do volunteer work in a developing country and help others. Imagine that your group is the Selection Committee. Your discussion group needs to choose one place for everyone to go for a year of study abroad.

Model Discussion

◆ *Choosing the Best Solution*

In this discussion, your group will decide where to go for its year abroad study program. Listen to the model discussion of one group of students as they identify criteria, list their options, and choose where to go for their year abroad.

Listening 1

Audio CD Track 38

◆ *Identifying the Criteria*

Listen and answer the following questions.
1. What criterion did they identify?
2. How did they define the criterion?

Listening 2

Audio CD Track 39

◆ *Listing the Options*

1. What three countries were suggested?

1._____

2._____

3._____

Listening 3

Audio CD Track 40

◆ *Choosing the Best Solution*

1. What was most important to each of the members of this discussion group? Complete the chart below.

Name	What's important to them?
Mary	
Richard	
Lou	
Phoebe	

◆ *Where do YOU want to go?*

Now it is your turn! Think about the countries you are interested in and think about what you would like to accomplish during your year abroad. Look to your values to help you come up with ideas for your discussion.

◆ **Prepare For Your Discussion**

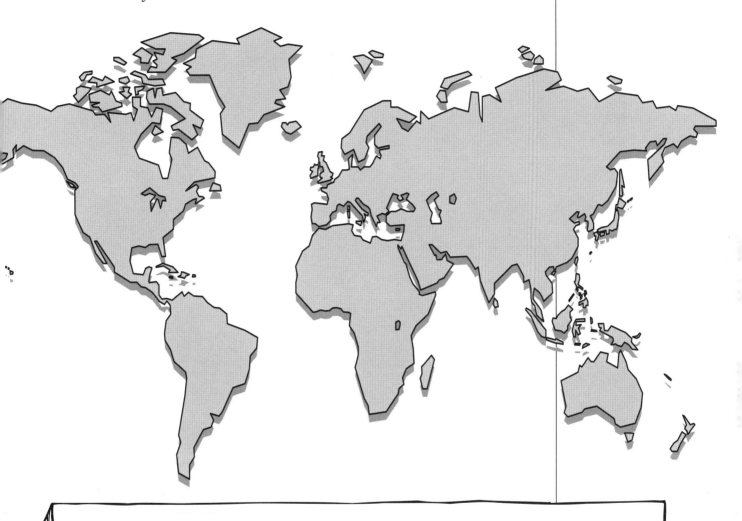

What countries are you interested in? _____

--------------------------------------- ---------------------------------------

--------------------------------------- ---------------------------------------

----

What would you like to accomplish during your year abroad? _____

Discussion Time!

Discussion Loop 7 ◆ *Choosing the Best Solution*

This loop is your discussion guide. The functions of this final Loop will help you make a decision about where to spend your year abroad.

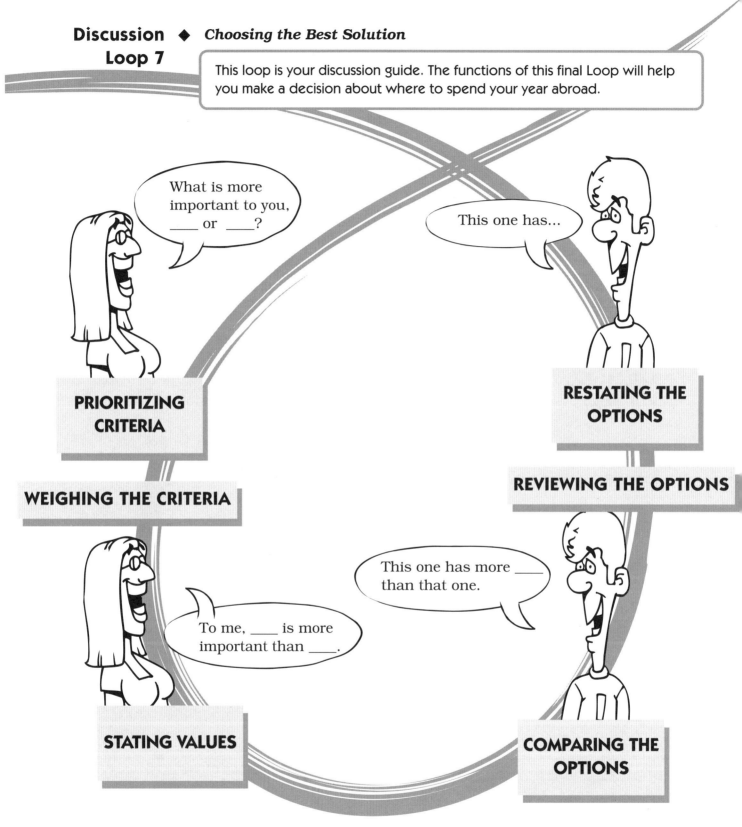

What is more important to you, ____ or ____?

This one has...

PRIORITIZING CRITERIA

RESTATING THE OPTIONS

WEIGHING THE CRITERIA

REVIEWING THE OPTIONS

This one has more ____ than that one.

To me, ____ is more important than ____.

STATING VALUES

COMPARING THE OPTIONS

Discussion Challenge
How many different phrases can you use from the Discussion Phrase Bank on page 108.

◆ *Identifying your Criteria*

Just as in Loops 5 and 6, in this discussion you will have to first brainstorm and identify your criteria for your year abroad. Then you will need to narrow and define those criteria.

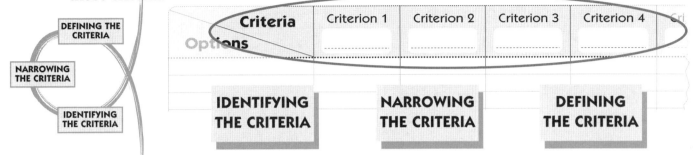

◆ *Listing your Options*

After you have identified your criteria you will need to brainstorm and suggest options the same as you did in Loop 6. Accept the options that best satisfy the criteria and reject the rest. Again, be sure to uncover your assumptions so that you find all of the best possible options.

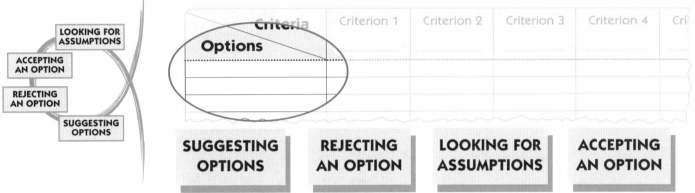

◆ *Choosing the Best Solution*

After you have identified your criteria and listed your options look to your values to help you choose the best solution. Weigh the criteria. Which criteria are most important to your group? What are your group's values? Carefully review each option comparing it with the other options. Finally, make your decision! Choose the best place for your group to spend their year abroad.

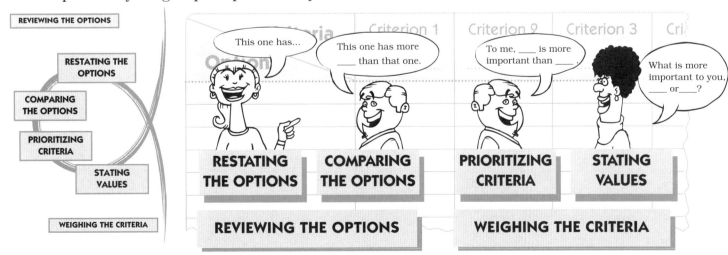

When everyone has competed this discussion task, turn the page and let's continue the discussion.

Option 1 ◆ *A Poster Presentation*

Step 1

Each group makes a poster.

Step 2

Affix the posters to the wall.

Step 3

Each group divides into visitors and booth personnel.

Step 4

Visitors check out the various booths while booth personnel remain at their booth to explain their choice to visitors.

Step 5

Each visitor votes for where they want to go for their year abroad.
Visitors cannot vote for their own booth's choice.

Step 6

Visitors and booth personnel switch roles and continue until everyone has had a chance to vote.

Read this before turning the page

This is your final discussion. At the end of this discussion, you will have the opportunity to do a self-assessment of your discussion ability. When you finish your self-assessment, you will be able to check the progress you have made by comparing this self-assessment to your first self-assessment.

◆ *Instructions*

1. Your teacher will explain the discussion background on page 116.
2. You will have 30 minutes for your discussion.
3. Be sure to use what you have learned in the 7 Loops and 7 Principles of discussion.
4. Take the self-assessment on page118.

Final Discussion:

Introducing Ourselves to Future Generations

Every generation is special and so is yours. What would you place in a time capsule to best represent your generation's values, likes, and beliefs?
In this final discussion, you will make a list of items to put into such a time capsule.

A Message To the Future

Time capsules are a way of communicating with future generations. The term Time Capsule was first used at the 1939 World's Fair in New York. A Time Capsule usually consists of a container that is filled with items that represent a certain place and time. The container is sealed for twenty, fifty, one hundred years or more. When it is opened, it serves as a window to the past. Imagine your discussion group is preparing a time capsule to be opened by students one hundred years from now. What items would you choose to put in a 60 cm square box that would best represent your world?

What goes into Your Time Capsule?

Get into small teams of 4 or 5 people. Discuss items to put into the time capsule. Remember, your items must fit into a 60 cm square box!

Finished? Now do the self-assessment on the next page.

Self-Assessment

◆ *How did you do?*

Congratulations! You have finished your final discussion. How do you feel about your performance in this discussion? Did you have a good time? How do you feel about your group's performance? Was it a good experience for everyone? Check your performance and your group's performance by taking this final self-assessment quiz.

Group Assessment

◆ *Group Assessment*

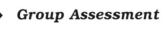

Group Assessment:

1. How active was your group?
   a. all group members participated about equally.
   b. some of the members did most of the talking.
   c. one person did most of the talking.
   d. we were silent most off the time.

2. Did your group encourage quiet, shy members to participate?
   a. There were no quiet or shy members in our group.
   b. Yes, we did
   c. No, we didn't
   d. I didn't notice.

3. How many items did your group come up with?
   a. 15 or more.
   b. 10 to 15.
   c. 5 to 10.
   d. less than 5

4. How many questions did your group ask each other?
   a. More than 10
   b. Between 5 and 10
   c. Between 1-5
   d. 0

5. Did your group finish the discussion within the time limit?
   a. Yes.
   b. We needed about 2 more minutes.
   c. We needed about 5 more minutes.
   d. We needed more than 5 minutes.

Individual Assessment:

1. How active were you?
   a. I did OK. I am satisfied with my participation.
   b. I should have talked more.
   c. I should have talked less and listened more.
   d. I was embarrassed by my English and didn't participate.

2. Did you encourage quiet, shy members to participate?
   a. There were no quiet or shy members in our group.
   b. Yes, I did.
   c. No, I didn't.
   d. I was a quiet, shy group member.

3. How many items did you suggest?
   a. I suggested 6 or more items
   b. I suggested three to five items.
   c. I suggested one or two items.
   d. None.

4. In this discussion, how many questions did you ask?
   a. More than 8
   b. Between 3 and 8
   c. 1 or 2
   d. 0

5. Did you take any notes during the discussion?
   a. I wrote down my ideas and everyone else's.
   b. I wrote down some ideas.
   c. I wrote down a few ideas.
   d. I didn't take any notes.

Now turn to page 124 for your Self-Assessment Scoring

Eastin

Listen to your groups' questions about the Eastin Hotel. Answer with the information from the box below. Then, ask your group members questions about the other hotels and complete the table below.

	Swimming Pool	Location	Room	Service Rating	Polynesian show and luau	Recreational Activities	Price
Eastin	1 pool, 60,000 sq. ft.	Only two blocks from beautiful Waikiki Beach	300 sq. ft.; Partial ocean view	3 Palm Tree Rating 🌴🌴🌴	20 minute show	Golf Tennis Hula lessons	$278 per night tax not included
Bilton							
Two Seasons							
HOLIDAY OUT							

Tell me about the pool!

How much does it cost?

How far is it from the beach?

What sort or recreational activities do they have?

Ask your group members questions about their hotels and complete the table below. Listen to their questions about the Bilton Hotel. Answer with the information from the box below.

Bilton

	Swimming Pool	Location	Room	Service Rating	Polynesian show and luau	Recreational Activities	Price
Eastin							
Bilton	2 pools 60,000 sq. ft.	5 minutes to the beach by free shuttle	400 sq. ft mountain view	3 Palm Tree Rating ❀❀❀	60 minute show drinks are extra	Golf and Tennis Free Hawaiian language lessons	$280 per night tax not included
Two Seasons							
Holiday Out							

Tell me about the pool!

How much does it cost?

How far is it from the beach?

What sort or recreational activities do they have?

Two Seasons

Ask your group members questions about their hotels and complete the table below. Listen to their questions about the The Two Seasons Hotel. Answer with the information from the box below.

	Swimming Pool	Location	Room	Service Rating	Polynesian show and luau	Recreational Activities	Price
Eastin							
Bilton							
Two Seasons	1 pool with water slide	Across the highway from the beach	200 sq. ft. Ocean view	4 Palm Tree Rating 🌴🌴🌴🌴	none	Golf Tennis Ping-Pong	$285 per night tax included
HOLIDAY OUT							

Tell me about the pool!

How much does it cost?

How far is it from the beach?

What sort of recreational activities do they have?

HOLIDAY OUT

Ask your group members questions about their hotels and complete the table below. Listen to their questions about the Holiday Out Hotel. Answer with the information from the box below.

	Swimming Pool	Location	Room	Service Rating	Polynesian show and luau	Recreational Activities	Price
Eastin							
Bilton							
Two Seasons							
HOLIDAY OUT	5 pools, total 85,000 sq. ft. 128 ft. water slide	On Waikiki Beach; only 5 minutes from shopping, dining and entertainment.	400 square ft. private balcony/lanai deluxe ocean view	5 Palm Tree Rating 🌴🌴🌴🌴🌴	90 minute show with all you can eat buffet	Surfing Scuba diving Snorkeling Windsurfing Hula lessons Golf Tennis	$280 per night tax included

What sort or recreational activities do they have?

How far is it from the beach?

How much does it cost?

Tell me about the pool!

Self-Assessment Scoring

Self-Assessment Scoring

◆ *Initial Self-Assessment Scoring*

Step 1: Scoring
Give yourself 4 points for every "a" answer you circled.
Give yourself 3 points for every "b" answer you circled.
Give yourself 2 points for every "c" answer you circled.
Give yourself 1 point for every "d" answer you circled.

Write your score here for the Group Assessment _____
Write your score here for the Individual Assessment _____

Step 2: Analysis
Compare your scores for the Group Assessment and the Individual Assessment.

If your Individual score is larger than your Group score:
Congratulations! You are a Strong Discussion Group Participant.

If your Individual score is the same as your Group score:
OK! You are an Average Discussion Group Participant.

If your Individual score is less than your Group score:
Try a little harder! You are a Weak Discussion Group Participant.

◆ *Final Self-Assessment Scoring*

Step 1: Scoring
Give yourself 4 points for every "a" answer you circled.
Give yourself 3 points for every "b" answer you circled.
Give yourself 2 points for every "c" answer you circled.
Give yourself 1 point for every "d" answer you circled.

Write your score here for the Group Assessment _____
Write your score here for the Individual Assessment _____

Step 2: Analysis
Compare your results with your initial self-assessment. Do you feel that you are a stronger participant now compared to your first discussion?

Answers ◆ *Answer to page 58 Problem 1*

1~16 (16 squares)   17~25 (9 squares)   26~29 (4 squares)   30 (1 square)

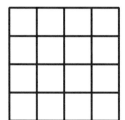
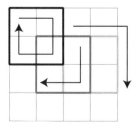
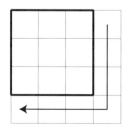
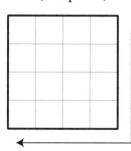

Total: 30 squares

◆ *Answer to page 58 Problem 2*

The sum of the angles of a spherical triangle can be anywhere between π and 3π radians or in other words between 180° and 540°. A spherical triangle is formed on the surface of a sphere by the intersection of 3 great arcs. The amount by which the sum of the angles exceeds 180° is called the spherical excess and is denoted E or Δ.

$$\Delta = R2[(A+B+C)-\pi] = R2E$$

◆ *Answer to page 86 Puzzle*

Start with your pencil at point 1 and draw a straight line to point 2 then without lifting your pencil draw a line at a 45° angle and continue past the 3 dot finally forming a right triangle. People tend to assume that the lines cannot go past the 3 dot that forms the box... thus when we do, we are thinking outside of the box.

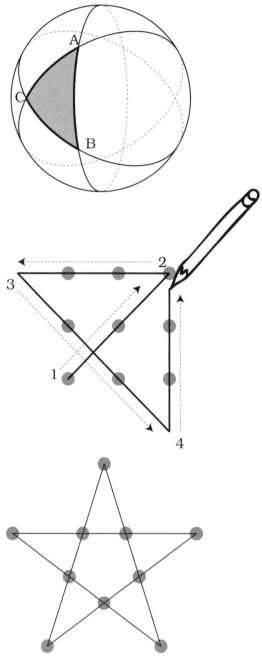

◆ *Answer to page 87 Puzzle*

There are several other asymmetrical possibilities as well. Can you find any of them?

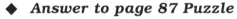

◆ *Answer to page 89 Puzzle*

Were you assuming that only the dimensions of length and width exist? By adding a 3rd dimension, height, we can configure the squares into one stack of four squares or two stacks of two squares. Can you think of any other 3 dimensional configurations?

This book is dedicated to our children:
Ray and Jay LeBeau
Kikiyo, Tsukasa, Tyler, and Kilan Harrington

Acknowledgments:

The legendary UCLA basketball coach, John Wooden, once said it takes 10 hands to make a basket. This is even truer for making a book. Language Solutions would like to thank the following people and organizations for their invaluable help during the writing of this book: The University of Oregon Academic Learning Services and the Eugene Public Library for help during the initial stages of the book. Gayle Pellicano, Miguel Sosa, Paul del Rosario for their corrections, ideas and inspiration. The flexible and accommodating staff at the Yokohama Bay Sheraton Hotel and Towers where the bulk of the first draft was written on consecutive weekends during 2005. Michael Woodrum and Soundmoves Studios in Hollywood California for an unforgettable recording experience. The staff at the Sheraton Universal Hotel and the Hilton Universal City and Towers for taking care of family and friends while we toiled in the studio. The staff at IPI for their interest and support for this book. The Japanese Association of Language Teachers, JALT, for its national conferences where this and other books started as but a glimmer in its authors' eyes.

A very special thank you goes to David's students at Ferris Women's University for their help in trialing these lessons;
Saori Aoyama, Aisa Kaku, Yurina Kuriyama, Erika Shinohara, Ai Sugiyama, Rie Nakashima, Yuka Hatakeyama, Sachi Hijikata, Aki Fujiwara, Chiaki Matsuda, Kanako Murayama, Airi Yamamoto, Ayako Yamamoto, Risa Yokohara, Ikuko Yoshida, Yuka Ishii, Nari Umeda, Yuki Ogura, Ayako Ozawa, Akari Koyama, Miho Kon, Mana Suzuki, Eri Nakada, Aki Mizukami, Yasuna Mizuta, Hiroko Minoda, Mai Momoi, Akiko Yoshioka, Kaori Adachi, Ayumi Ota, Mayumi Kiyono, Kaoru Koshiishi, Risa Sakai, Tomoko Sanada, Miki Takeuchi, Risa Terashima, Yuka Nagasawa, Chieko Nakamura, Tomomi Nakayama, Saori Hamada, Yuki Maruyama, Sayaka Mizunuma, Mina Yoshida, and Ayako Yoshino

Charles LeBeau would like to thank: Bill, Satoru, and Angelo in Tokyo, and Bob, Gus, Jenny and Jerry, and Sue in Eugene. In addition, a special thank you to Rieko for her friendship, and to my students at Yokohama City University and at Kyoritsu Women's University. And most of all my family: my brothers who put up with me; my sons who inspire me; and my wife who lovesall of me, the good and the bad.

David Harrington would like to thank: Mami Ushida Harrington, Kikiyo Marie Harrington, Tsukasa James Harrington, Tyler Patrick Harrington, and Kilan Masami Harrington for teaching me what love has to do with it.

Hiroaki Kawajiri would like to thank: Kyoji and Masumi Udo (my wife's parents) and my parents for taking care of my family while I was away from home for this project. Shoko Udo, Nami Udo (7) and Fuki Udo (5) for being with me as part of my life.